RAYMOND D'AGUILERS

Memoirs of the
AMERICAN PHILOSOPHICAL SOCIETY
Held at Philadelphia
For Promoting Useful Knowledge
Volume 71

RAYMOND D'AGUILERS

Historia Francorum Qui Ceperunt Iherusalem

Translated with Introduction and Notes by

JOHN HUGH HILL and LAURITA L. HILL

Department of History
University of Houston

THE AMERICAN PHILOSOPHICAL SOCIETY
INDEPENDENCE SQUARE ● PHILADELPHIA
1968

Library of Congress Catalog
Card Number 68-24358

FOREWORD

In the course of our research in the First Crusade we became interested in the history of Raymond d'Aguilers titled *Historia Francorum qui ceperunt Iherusalem.* The initial encouragement for this translation came from the late Professor A. C. Krey. In the course of our studies we also turned to the publication of a text based on MS. Latin 14,378, Bibliothèque Nationale, Paris (formerly of Saint-Victor of Paris).

We are indebted to many agencies and people for the completion of our text and translation. The American Philosophical Society has been most generous in assisting us in our research in Europe as well as in the United States. Libraries have been helpful in many ways. We acknowledge the assistance of the following: The Bibliothèque Nationale and the Bibliothèque de l'Arsenal of Paris, the Bibliothèque Municipale de Clermont-Ferrand, the Bibliothèque Municipale de Toulouse, the Bibliothèque de l'Institut d'Études méridionales de la Faculté des lettres et sciences humaines de Toulouse, the British Museum, the Burgerbibliothek of Berne, and the libraries of the University of Houston, the University of Texas, and Texas Agricultural and Mechanical University.

We are particularly grateful to several European scholars who have separated our scholarship from our locale, and whose interest has stimulated us to further research. We acknowledge our debt to our good friends, Professor Philippe Wolff of the University of Toulouse, Professor Jean Richard of the University of Dijon, and Dr. Hans E. Mayer of the Monumenta Germaniae Historica.

We again recognize the interest and encouragement throughout many years of the late Professors Frederic Duncalf and A. C. Krey. We are also appreciative of the assistance of Professors Marshall W. Baldwin, J. A. Brundage, Harold S. Fink, A. R. Lewis, and Robert S. Lopez. We have also received support from administrative officials in the University of Houston. Last but not least we are grateful to Raymond d'Aguilers who wrote *Historia Francorum qui ceperunt Iherusalem* and thereby furnished us many pleasant hours.

JOHN HUGH AND LAURITA L. HILL

CONTENTS

ILLUSTRATIONS

RAYMOND D'AGUILERS

INTRODUCTION

The crusades have continued to attract interest despite the fact that Professor LaMonte wrote several years ago that in the light of other fields of medieval history they were overworked.[1] Only recently Hans Eberhard Mayer in his excellent bibliography of the crusades, *Bibliographie zur Geschichte der Kreuzzüge,* listed 5,362 works written in that area of study to 1958.[2] In retrospect, we realize that Pope Urban had no idea of the scholarly impact of his speech of November 27, 1095, delivered before a crowd assembled on the undulating hills surrounding Clermont.[3] But the launching of a semi-barbaric world of Latins against the Islamic community caught the fancy of posterity. Historians, poets, novelists, pyschologists, and even captains of modern cinema responded to the emotional pull of this unusual movement in history. The aura of romanticism and lofty idealism associated with crusading lingers in the twentieth century and the word "crusade" is still loosely applied by conflicting ideologies.

Pope Urban's call initiated the First Crusade, the most successful and the most discussed of the many ensuing crusades. The motives of Pope Urban have been widely explored and his plans still evoke scholarly disputation.[4] Likewise the antecedents of the crusades as well as underlying forces of motivation have been argued.[5] Historians have also given attention

[1] John L. LaMonte, "Some Problems in Crusading Historiography," *Speculum* **15** (1940): pp. 57-75.

[2] Hans E. Mayer, *Bibliographie zur Geschichte der Kreuzzüge* (Hannover, 1960).

[3] D. C. Munro, "The Speech of Pope Urban II at Clermont, 1095," *American Historical Review* **11** (1906): pp. 231-242. Frederic Duncalf, "The Councils of Piacenza and Clermont," *A History of the Crusades* **1** (Philadelphia, 1955): pp. 237-247.

[4] M. W. Baldwin, "Some Recent Interpretations of Pope Urban's Eastern Policy," *Catholic Hist. Rev.* **25** (1940): pp. 459-466. A. C. Krey, "Urban's Crusade—Success or Failure," *Amer. Hist. Rev.* **53** (1948): pp. 235-250. Frederic Duncalf in a footnote, p. 221, in *A History of the Crusades* offers a comprehensive bibliography of literature on this subject. See James A. Brundage, "Recent Crusade Historiography: Some Observations and Suggestions," *Catholic Hist. Rev.* **49** (1964): pp. 493-507. Part of this preface is drawn from a paper read by John Hugh Hill on "Revisions in the History of the First Crusade." at a session of the American Historical Association in Washington in 1961.

[5] P. Alphandéry and A. Dupront, *La Chrétienté et l'idée de croisade* (Paris, 1954). C. Erdmann, *Die Entstehung des Kreuzzugsgedankens* (Stuttgart, 1935). P.

to many facets of the First Crusade including military affairs, routes of the crusaders, sequence of events, and the leaders.[6] Furthermore, the interest has not been confined to any one country although France and Germany pioneered in the field. In the United States the zeal of Professor D. C. Munro and his continuators led to such productivity that Steven Runciman deplored competition with the "massed typewriters" of this country.[7]

Despite the plethora of writing, much remains to be done.[8] This need of continued study stems from the frequent misuse of the available source material plus the compounding of errors by historians who have refused to enlist the services of specialists in allied fields. In addition, twentieth-century historians have attempted to fit their theories of human motivation upon the materials of the First Crusade. Furthermore, our shortage of materials stems from the apocalyptic outlook taken by its chroniclers. From the beginning of the crusade the writers were more concerned with the ways of God than with the ways of man. The beginner is always shocked by the fact that the monastic records are so scanty. A few lines on the conquest of Jerusalem in an annal compete with several lines giving an account of falling stars. If any credence in annals can be given, then they reveal that the importance of the crusade dawned on people after the capture of Jerusalem and the reports of returning crusaders sifted into Europe. If then the monasteries fail us to what sources can we turn?

Rousset, *Les Origines et les caractères de la première croisade* (Neuchâtel, 1954). M. Villey, *La Croisade: Essai sur la formation d'une théorie juridique* (Paris, 1942).

[6] R. C. Smail, *Crusading Warfare (1097-1193). A Contribution to Medieval Military History* (Cambridge, 1956). Heinrich Hagenmeyer, "Chronologie de la première croisade," *Revue de l'Orient Latin* 6-8 (1898-1901). J. C. Andressohn, *The Ancestry and Life of Godfrey of Bouillon* (Bloomington, 1947). Charles W. David, *Robert Curthose, Duke of Normandy* (Cambridge, 1920). John Hugh Hill and Laurita L. Hill, *Raymond IV de Saint-Gilles* (Toulouse, 1959), and translation, *Raymond IV, Count of Toulouse* (Syracuse, 1962). Marshall M. Knappen, "Robert II of Flanders in the First Crusade," *The Crusades and other Historical Essays Presented to Dana C. Munro* (New York, 1928): pp. 79-100. Robert Lawrence Nicholson, *Tancred: A Study of His Career and Work in Their Relation to the First Crusade and the Establishment of the Latin States in Syria and Palestine* (Chicago, 1940). R. B. Yewdale, *Bohemond I, Prince of Antioch* (Princeton, 1917).

[7] Steven Runciman, *A History of the Crusades* 1 (Cambridge, 1951).

[8] A. S. Atiya, *The Crusade: Historiography and Bibliography* (Bloomington, 1962).

Fortunately we have a number of extant eyewitness accounts. In the light of modern reporting they are totally inadequate and filled with church lore, but compared with earlier periods in the Middle Ages these eyewitness reports are more numerous and informative. Perhaps the most neglected area of study includes the origins of the crusades and the plans of Urban. Modern historians have largely argued *ex silentio*.[9] The historian fares better when he comes to the actual conduct of the First Crusade. There are a number of available letters ranging from letters of popes, the Emperor Alexius, and the leaders of the crusades to the poignant letters of Stephen of Blois to his wife Adela.[10] At best these documents are short and contain fewer words than a morning report of an army company. However, they are factual and one of our best sources of information.

Historians are fortunate in having five full-length Greek or Latin histories written by so-called eyewitnesses. Fulcher, a native of Chartres, started his crusading journey with Robert of Normandy and Stephen of Blois. He later joined forces with Baldwin, the brother of Godfrey of Bouillon, and became his chaplain. His history, *Historia Hierosolymitana,* was written in installments, the first one of which deals primarily with the First Crusade. This work composed probably in 1101 carries the reader to Edessa because it was here that Fulcher abandoned the crusade. His account of the completion of the journey was not a first-hand account.[11] Anna Comnena, the daughter of the Emperor Alexius Comnenus, wrote the *Alexiad.* Written some forty years after the First Crusade, this account deals

9 Frederic Duncalf, "The Pope's Plan for the First Crusade," *The Crusades and other Historical Essays Presented to Dana C. Munro* (New York, 1928): pp. 44-56.

10 Heinrich Hagenmeyer, *Die Kreuzzugsbriefe aus den Jahren 1088-1100* (Innsbruck, 1901). P. Riant, "Inventaire critique des lettres historiques des croisades," *Archives de l'Orient Latin* 1 (1881).

11 Fulcherius Carnotensis, *Historia Hierosolymitana Gesta Francorum Iherusalem Peregrinantium* in *Recueil des historiens des croisades: historiens occidentaux* 3 (Paris, 1866) (hereafter cited as *RHC Occ.*); *Historia Hierosolymitana. Gesta Francorum Iherusalem Peregrinantium* (ed. Heinrich Hagenmeyer, Heidelberg, 1913). Mary E. McGinty, *Fulcher of Chartres, Chronicle of the First Crusade* (Philadelphia, 1941). This is a partial translation of Fulcher. Harold S. Fink is working on a complete translation. Some historians believe that Fulcher started his history in 1101. If he did begin his work in that year it would indicate that the work of Raymond d'Aguilers was completed. However, we have no absolute proof.

primarily with the role of her father and is far from dependable. Anna was a young person at the time of the crusade and in retrospect confused chronology and many events.[12]

Peter Tudebode, a priest of Civray, wrote before 1111 the *Historia de Hierosolymitano itinere* which for many years was considered an important eyewitness history. It is, no doubt, true that he was present on the journey to Jerusalem, but modern scholars have relegated his work to that of a plagiarism, primarily of the anonymous history, titled the *Gesta*, with borrowings from the narrative of Raymond d'Aguilers.[13] Certainly to all intents and purposes the information in his history and that of the *Gesta* are close, and for our study we can state that there are two very important eyewitness accounts for following the First Crusade from its inception to its successful conclusion, namely those of the author of the *Gesta* and of Raymond d'Aguilers.

The most studied and best understood of these two histories is that one titled the *Gesta*. The anonymous writer followed Bohemond to Antioch and continued the journey to Jerusalem after the Norman lingered in Antioch along with other crusaders. Since the studies of Sybel much research has been done on this source. Scholars have not been able to agree on many phases of the problem. The anonymous author remains so, and although Runciman assigns the completion of the *Gesta* in 1100 or 1101 that also is unsolved. The list of scholars who have turned their minds to his work include Hagenmayer, Bréhier, Lees, and Hill to mention only a few.[14]

Oddly enough, the remaining source titled *Historia Francorum qui ceperunt Iherusalem* has attracted no such attention. If this is true concerning research on the author and his methods, it is also true in regard to the inadequacies of present texts which have been deplored by Runciman.[15] Any serious

---

[12] Anna Comnena, *Alexiade* (ed. B. Leib), in *Collection byzantine de l'Association Guillaume Budé* (Paris, 1937-1945). E. A. S. Dawes, *The Alexiad of the Princess Anna Comnena* (London, 1928).

[13] Petrus Tudebodus, *Historia de Hierosolymitano itinere,* in *RHC Occ* **3** (Paris, 1866).

[14] Heinrich Hagenmeyer, *Anonymi gesta Francorum et aliorum Hierosolimitanorum* (Heidelberg, 1890). Louis Bréhier, *Histoire anonyme de la première croisade* in *Les Classiques de l'histoire de France au Moyen Age,* **4** (Paris, 1924). See Mayer, *Bibliographie* for other editions and critical works, p. 49.

[15] Runciman, *op. cit.,* p. 329, n. 1. Our forthcoming text of Raymond d'Aguilers will be published in "Documents relatifs à l'histoire des croisades" (l'Académie

scholar of the First Crusade must deal with the history of
Raymond d'Aguilers which is extremely important in historiography of the crusades. Although his work parallels the *Gesta*,
at times it furnishes information not available in other histories.
Raymond provides details of the Provençal journey to Constantinople which are lacking in accounts other than that of
Tudebode. He also deals more adequately with the shadowy
figure of Adhémar, Bishop of Le Puy, than does the anonymous
author of the *Gesta*. His account of the journey from Constantinople to Antioch is very sketchy, but nevertheless contains some additional information. His story of the siege of
Antioch, although confused in chronology at times, adds sub-
stantially to our knowledge. His description of events from
the fall of Antioch to the abandonment of the siege of 'Arqah
is important, especially his account of the Trial of the Holy
Lance, which is strangely missing in the *Gesta*. His information concerning the church quarrels after the fall of Jerusalem
fills the lacuna left by the *Gesta*.

In short, the history of Raymond d'Aguilers must be used.
William of Tyre, one of the most celebrated armchair historians
of the First Crusade, had to use his work, and so have other
historians.[16] While historians have learned that they must live
with the chaplain, they also learned that they had a contract
with a medieval Baron Munchausen who swore to be a faithful
reporter, but more than likely combined fact and fiction with
the greatest of ease. In their frustrations they often misunder-
stood Raymond d'Aguilers because of the very obscurity of
his life. Actually what do we know of this raconteur, this
spinner of tall crusading tales? Alas, we have to depend upon
his book and internal criticism for our information.

des Inscriptions et Belles Lettres). Raimundus de Aguilers, *Historia Francorum
qui ceperunt Iherusalem* in *RHC Occ* 3 (Paris, 1866). See A. C. Krey, *The First
Crusade* (Princeton, 1921). Krey has translated a number of sources and has
combined them in a narrative of the First Crusade. See also M. Guizot's translation of Raymond's history in *Collection des memoires relatif à l'histoire de
France*. No. 21 (Paris, 1824). Guizot does not give a critical translation and notes.
    16 Willelmus Tyrensis archiepiscopus, *Historia rerum in partibus transmarinis
gestarum* in *RHC Occ* 1 (Paris, 1844). William of Tyre, *A History of Deeds
Done Beyond the Seas*, translated by E. A. Babcock and A. C. Krey, 1 (New
York, 1943). Albertus Aquensis, *Historia Hierosolymitana* in *RHC Occ* 4 (Paris,
1879). William was influenced by the history of Albert.

THE AUTHOR

Raymond d'Aguilers, self-styled author of *Historia Francorum qui ceperunt Iherusalem,* so far as his life is concerned has left a cold trail. We first made his acquaintance two decades ago when we were working on a revisionist biography of Raymond of Saint-Gilles.[17] If we can believe him, he was a chaplain of Count Raymond IV of Toulouse, accompanied the count on the crusade, and was made a priest on the journey. He refers to himself as a canon of Le Puy and his history as a book written for the information of the Bishop of Viviers.[18] Le Puy, picturesque with its volcanic formations, was the center of considerable religious activity before the First Crusade. Bishop Adhémar of Le Puy met Pope Urban II there on August 15, 1095, and became closely attached to papal plans for the crusade.[19] The abbey of Chaise-Dieu, one of the favorite places of worship for the Count of Toulouse, was also close.[20] As a traveler views Chapelle St. Michel-d'Aiguilhe today and the battlements of the counts of Polignac en route to Chaise-Dieu, he may be tempted to think that the environment was appropriate for the training of a chronicler of Holy War.[21]

However, the most simple details of Raymond's life are missing, and no record of the dates of his birth and death exists. The major manuscripts give the following variants of his name—Agilers, Agiles, Aguilers, and Aguillers. These spelling variants are purely scribal and have no significance. It is possible that he came from the Department of Haute-Loire as Runciman has suggested, but again such is purely conjectural.[22]

[17] John Hugh Hill and Laurita L. Hill, *Raymond IV de Saint-Gilles,* see n. 6.
[18] This information is drawn from Raymond's introduction. See p. 15.
[19] John Hugh Hill and Laurita L. Hill, "Contemporary Accounts and the Later Reputation of Adhémar, Bishop of Puy," *Medievalia et Humanistica* **9** (1955): pp. 30-38. This article provoked a lively controversy when James A. Brundage wrote "Adhémar of Puy and His Critics," *Speculum* **34** (1959): pp. 201-212. See also Hans Eberhard Mayer, "Zur Beurteilung Adhemars von Le Puy," *Deutsches Archiv* **16** (1960) and Jean Richard's discussion in *Journal des Savants,* 1960-1961.
[20] Pierre-Roger Gaussin, *L'Abbaye de la Chaise-Dieu (1043-1158)* (Paris, 1960). This excellent work points out the influence of Chaise-Dieu in the life of Raymond of Saint-Gilles; see pp. 130-132.
[21] *Ibid,* pp. 70-72.
[22] Runciman, *op. cit.,* p. 328.

We prefer to think of him in connection with the picturesque Church of the Needle of Le Puy, but the evidence is lacking.

If details of his life are scanty so are facts concerning the composition of his history. Raymond relates that he undertook his study as a joint project with Pons of Balazun, who was an obscure knight in the entourage of Raymond of Saint-Gilles. He also relates that the work was undertaken to allay criticism of the crusade as well as to show the glory and justice of God's ways. Raymond indicates that he knows more than he relates but that he prefers to devote his time to the activities of forces of Count Raymond IV of Toulouse. His fellow historian, Pons, fell victim to battle wounds at 'Arqah and left the work of completion to the chaplain.[23] Runciman thinks that Raymond completed his work in 1099 but in this he errs, because as we have mentioned above the author was cognizant of the impact of the cynicism which followed the conquest of Jerusalem. Perhaps Krey is more nearly correct in assuming that the work was finished by 1102, but we can only be certain that it was complete before the death of Raymond of Toulouse.[24] His work shows that he compiled his story by using his own notes, personal experiences, and other available histories. All evidence points to the fact that he arranged his materials after the events. Unfortunately, the original manuscript is lost and the two oldest manuscripts are mid-twelfth century.[25]

Happily, Raymond's book reveals many facts concerning the man, his education, his tastes, his feelings, and his prejudices. In a review of our book on Raymond of Saint-Gilles, Steven Runciman wrote that we thought that the chaplain was stupid, inaccurate, and prejudiced.[26] We intended to give the impression that the chaplain was superstitious, prejudiced, and careless in matters of minutiae, but we did not intend to convey the idea that he was stupid. Raymond was honest in the sense

---

[23] See p. 15.

[24] Runciman, *op. cit.*, p. 328. A. C. Krey, *The First Crusade*, p. 9. See n. 15.

[25] We have not included readings from MS Latin 5131A, Bibliothèque Nationale, Paris, fifteenth century, because it is late and attempts to combine Fulcher and Raymond, nor from MS Latin 5132 (noted by the *Recueil* but late fourteenth century and incomplete). MS Latin 6041 A, Bibliothèque Nationale, Paris, is late and incomplete. British Museum, MS Harley 4340 is mislabeled and is not Raymond's book.

[26] Steven Runciman has a book review of *Raymond IV de Saint-Gilles* in *English Hist. Rev.* (July, 1961): pp. 515-516.

that he admitted his shortcomings, but like most writers of his time he was not averse to plagiarizing without any twinges of conscience. He was forthright in that he was an apologist for God, the Count of Toulouse, and the Christian militia. But the good canon had certain biases that are easy to detect. As did many clerics of his time, he placed the responsibility for military reverses upon prostitutes. Likewise, he hated the Greeks and made no effort to give them credit for aiding the cause. Prone to exaggerate the crusader's prowess, Raymond also colored descriptions of battles with ritualistic materials and loved to introduce miracles to liven up the dull events of daily life. His use of hagiographical materials points to his cleverness rather than to his naïveté. But above all he reveals a certain sensitivity to the events around him and at times shocks his reader by posing questions concerning the validity of the crusades.

In all, Raymond's history reveals a man of moderate education, well versed in church liturgy and imbued with pragmatic views of the ultimate triumph of Christianity, a man who compressed events of the First Crusade into a didactic history which has confused as much as it has enlightened. In short, judging by modern standards of biography, we know very little concerning Raymond d'Aguilers. Unfortunately, this unsatisfactory lack of information applies also to the manuscript tradition of his book.

MANUSCRIPT TRADITION

There are seven extant complete or nearly complete manuscripts of Raymond's book, as well as several fragmentary or garbled accounts. The manuscript which we chose to translate is the beautiful Saint Victor codex, better known as MS Latin 14,378, now of the Bibliothèque Nationale of Paris. This manuscript contains, in the order named, the works of Fulcher of Chartres, Walter the Chancellor, and Raymond d'Aguilers; this last named work was added, we are advised, because the account went into more detail than did the history of Fulcher. Occurring also in combination with the histories of Fulcher and

Walter the Chancellor are copies of Raymond's book found in MS Latin 5131 also of the Bibliothèque Nationale, Paris, MS Latin 1102, Bibliothèque de l'Arsenal, Paris, MS Latin 262, Bibliothèque de la Ville, Clermont-Ferrand, MS Latin 261 of the Burgerbibliotek, Berne, and MS Latin Additional 8927 of the British Museum. MS Latin 5511A of the Bibliothèque Nationale, Paris, contains only the work of Raymond and gives the title, *Historia Francorum qui ceperunt Iherusalem.*

In the printed tradition of Raymond's work, Bongars at the beginning of the seventeenth century included the history in his *Gesta Dei per Francos,* using a now lost manuscript, apparently a recension of the type represented by MS Latin 5511A and the Berne manuscript, MS Latin 261. Although Bongars used this lost manuscript as a basis for his edition, we do not have the exact readings of this lost work because, in his effort to establish a text from his two sources, he used emendations and introduced readings from MS Latin 261. We do know that the Bongars manuscript had lost the folios containing the account of the battle of Ascalon and that the scribe of the manuscript had copied the account from another author.

In 1866 a text of Raymond's history was published in the *Recueil des historiens des croisades.* MS Latin 14,378 was used as a basis with emendations drawn from MS Latin 5131, MS Latin 5511A, MS Latin 1102, and MS Latin 262. The Berne and London manuscripts were not used in this edition, although variants from Bongars, many of which followed MS Latin 261, Berne, were cited. Likewise the translations of his work have carried little or no critical material, and nothing significant has been done on his method since the monograph of Clemens Klein.[27]

In our study of the manuscripts, the printed editions, and the criticism of Raymond's work, we came to the conclusion that the methods followed by these critics and scholars could develop little new in the field. The printed editions had modernized punctuation and otherwise obscured the evidence of the scribes by changing manuscript divisions and emending at will and sometimes without notice. Literary allusions, para-

---

[27] See n. 15, also Clemens Klein, *Raimund von Aguilers, Quellenstudie zur Geschichte des ersten Kreuzzuges* (Berlin, 1892).

phrases, and parallels were often ignored as well as quotations from Biblical and liturgical sources.

Seeking then a means to develop more fruitful methods of gleaning information from these sources, we returned to the manuscripts for further study. Abandoning the effort to establish the readings of the lost original, we turned to the Saint-Victor manuscript, a complete and carefully edited edition of Raymond's work, as it remains to us today. In editing the work, we followed the pointing of the manuscript (a medieval guide for the rise and fall of the voice while reading out loud) and we sought textual enlightenment in the sources and models probably known to the author, the materials of his service books. The present translation, based upon our edition of the text of MS Latin 14,378 of the Bibliothèque Nationale, thus has abandoned the printed sources and reflects what we have learned from manuscript comparison and study. It became inescapable that, in the process of study of the manuscript tradition along with the translation of Raymond's history, we would learn his style and method, and in turning to this topic we must state that he was a clever writer who liked to make fiction appear factual.

STYLE AND METHOD

In chronology and detailed information Raymond's work leaves much to be desired, and in parallels with the *Gesta* his method reveals that he resorted to the use of information other than his own. Of course, purists are likely to belittle his work because his Latin compares unfavorably with that of Guibert, William of Tyre, and other writers more concerned with style than was the chaplain. But we cannot refrain from commenting that style in itself may obscure the truth.[28] Yet Raymond has a certain literary flair for description. Some of his passages reflect a sensitivity to his surroundings and thereby catch the spirit of crusading. His Latin is expressive and often reveals more pathos and human feeling than the stilted style of writers striving for literary effect. However, the reader will soon dis-

[28] Krey, *The First Crusade,* p. 8.

cover that the chaplain was, as he honestly confesses, a simple
churchman who knew little more than his service books and
religious matters pertaining to his office. Whatever classical
allusions appear in his work are usually derived from church
ritual. So it is to this ornamentation of his work that we now
turn in order that his history can be read with understanding.

This ornamentation has gone unnoticed by many scholars,
but a casual study of Raymond's history presents us with a
large body of borrowings from ritual, a characteristic which
the other accounts exhibit to a lesser degree and one to which
Bréhier has given some slight notice.[29] Raymond's language
is reminiscent of Psalms; his sequences relating to penance of
the army seem to be inspired at times by the collects. He
borrows freely from the Apochrypha, the miracles, and the
lives of saints. Modern historians still repeat his bloody account
of the Christian seizure of the Temple of Solomon in Jerusalem,
apparently without knowing that Raymond has caused them to
repeat a passage from Revelations.[30]

Raymond includes a hymn with rubrics, and at times adopts
a homiletic tone for a discourse upon the sins of the crusaders.
He does not hesitate to use a response to describe knights in
battle. He likewise uses the versicle, "Exsurge, Christi," and
the response "Et libera nos" when the Christians are ambushed.
He employs the versicle, "Vos omnes," and an antiphon to
promise the aid of the Lord. From these few examples we
like to picture the chaplain sitting at his desk surrounded by
his service books, which included a copy of the History of
the Maccabees, and perhaps with a common source of the
crusades, suffering from the heat and the cold while he explained to skeptics the mysterious ways of God, and finally
giving a sigh of relief when he "happily ended his book." [31]

Thus faced with this abundance of liturgical material, we
must perforce, as we have noticed before, regard Raymond
as a compiler, and as such, he displays literary ability and
education. He understands the accepted form of a style best
described by Professor Rudolph Willard as ecclesiastical fiction,
and he shows remarkable ability to combine facts rooted in

[29] Louis Bréhier, op. cit., p. 131, n. 4.

[30] See p. 127.

[31] The sources of these various forms will be given in the footnotes of the
translation. See page 35 for a good example.

moral and religious imagery.[32] His skill in this matter has enabled him to make dupes of many historians. His story is well framed with attention to design. Coming events cast their shadows before, thus revealing that his literary aspirations outstrip his desire to record a day by day account as he journeyed to Jerusalem. He borrows tags from the classics probably by the way of church materials and particularly from his knowledge of Ambrose. Nevertheless, he uses them appropriately for descriptive values and appreciates their beauty.

The author uses the Gospels to dictate the justice of the occasion and makes an effort to bring his account into earthly setting. The truth of the miracle is attested by two or more witnesses as in homily and the Old and the New Testaments. Peter Bartholomew, the discoverer of the Holy Lance, was slightly burned in the ordeal fire because of his early doubts concerning the Lance. His entire story concerning the Lance together with all of its ramifications represents a clever fabrication. Even in his description of the garb of the heavenly visitors, the good canon is careful to give details based upon current iconographic patterns of the period.[33]

Further, Raymond used a literary device which became popular years later when the humanists would display their knowledge of Latin by hurling invectives against an imaginary enemy, thereby leading their readers to await eagerly the name of the poor fellow and at the last moment denying their audience the pleasure of such a disclosure by writing, "Heaven forbid." In the case of Raymond, he will take his readers to the very threshold of the brothel, the dalliances of the dancing girls, and the rape of screaming women, but he will stop short, leaving his audience to their imagination. On the other hand he rather enjoys describing revolting acts of bloodshed and narrates them with relish.

At times Raymond reveals a literary flair as evidenced by a few examples. He mentions the clashes of the Byzantines and the Provençals very briefly, then hurries to inform his readers,

Shall I write of the most fraudulent and abominable treachery of the Emperor's counsel? Or shall I record the most infamous escape

---

[32] Rudolph Willard, *Two Apocrypha in Old English Homilies* in *Beiträge zur Englischen Philologie* **30** (1935): p. 2.

[33] See translation, pp. 100-102. The ordeal fire refers to the ordeal which Peter Bartholomew underwent at 'Arqah.

of our army and its unimaginable helplessness? Or by relating the deaths of such great princes, shall I leave a memorial of eternal grief? To the contrary, let whoever wishes to know inquire from others rather than from us.[34]

Like many medieval writers, Raymond excelled in descriptive writing as revealed in a few of the following passages. After the victory of the Count of Flanders near Antioch, the chaplain relates that one could see the "slain lying along the way like sheaves of grain at harvest time." [35] Raymond exults following the defeat of the Tripolitans by writing, "It was a delightful sight as the swirling waters of the aqueduct tumbled the headless bodies of nobles and rabble into Tripoli." [36] He likewise makes sin unprofitable when he relates the death of Turkish horsemen as they plunged from a sheer precipice to escape pursuing crusaders. He thinks that this was a pleasing sight to God; but the loss of the horses was a disturbing thought to the chaplain.[37] Forewarned by such knowledge the reader may study Raymond's history critically, at all times remembering that the author takes the teleological approach to history. Thus Raymond's book poses not only the problem of understanding his method but also the question of the translation of his history so as to bring him into the twentieth century without doing violence to his opus.

THE TRANSLATION

We undertook this translation several years ago largely owing to the support which we received from the American Philosophical Society in the form of three grants. We also received aid from Texas Agricultural and Mechanical University and the University of Houston. In the course of our efforts we have made many translations and revisions. Finally, after some soul searching, we decided to make a free translation and thus subject ourselves to possible criticism from

[34] See p. 22-23.
[35] See p. 35.
[36] See p. 105.
[37] See p. 48.

purists. After the initial plunge we felt that we had recaptured somewhat the spirit of Raymond and made his history a part of man's history rather than a dry antique reserved for Latinists. In doing so we have abandoned Elizabethan expressions which so often dot medieval translations. We have omitted "thee" and "thou," and we have taken many liberties with construction in the interest of clarity. Like all translations, there will undoubtedly be errors which will make a reviewer happy. But we hope that the reader will be more concerned with the flow of the narrative, a story touched by the pathos of an ignorant group of Latins who undertook a journey to recover the Holy Sepulchre. In his simple style Raymond revealed their hopes, fears, and joys, and recorded the despair of the weak, the heroism of those killed in battle, the expectations of a heavenly reward, and the questioning of the human heart which asks why is war God's plan.

The History of Frankish Conquerors of Jerusalem

By Raymond d'Aguilers, Canon of Notre Dame du Puy

Pons of Balazun [1] and Raymond, Canon of Le Puy,[2] pray to you my lord, Bishop of Viviers,[3] and to all of the orthodox for your blessing and sharing in our toil. We write this book in order to inform you and all the people beyond the Alps of the mighty works which God in his customary generosity incessantly brought to pass through us. This task, chiefly undertaken because misfits of war and cowardly deserters have since tried to spread lies rather than truth, shall enable future readers to avoid the friendship and counsel of such renegades because their works will be an open book. It is a matter of record that God's army, although it bore the whip of the Lord for its transgressions, nevertheless triumphed over all paganism because of His loving kindness. But it seems too tiresome to write of each journey since some crusaders went through Sclavonia,[4] others by Hungary,[5] by Lombardy, or by the sea. So, we have taken care to write of the Count of Saint-Gilles,[6] the Bishop of Le Puy,[7] and their army without bothering with the others.

[1] Pons of Balazun, joint author of Raymond's book, was probably a knight from the diocese of Viviers. There are several variants of his name, including Balon, Ballon, and Baladun. He was killed during the siege of 'Arqah, and Raymond completed the book.

[2] Raymond, Canon of Le Puy, was author of *Historia Francorum qui ceperunt Iherusalem*. See preface; also Runciman, *op. cit.*, pp. 328-329.

[3] The Bishop of Viviers at the time of the First Crusade was Leger. Viviers was southeast of Le Puy and Chaise-Dieu. It was closely associated with Chaise-Dieu which was a favorite abbey of Raymond of Toulouse. See Dom. Cl. Devic and Dom. J. Vaisette, *Histoire générale de Languedoc* (15 v., Paris, 1872-1893) **3**: p. 542. Hereafter cited as *HGL*.

[4] Sclavonia is Raymond's word for Dalmatia, the land of the Slavs. His description of Sclavonia as a "forsaken land, both inaccessible and mountainous" is probably drawn from Psalm 62:3. This Psalm. "Deus, Deus, Meus," occurs in the Office Sunday at Laudes, in the Office of the Dead at Laudes, and on such other occasions as the Breviary calls for the Psalms of Sunday.

[5] Hungary had experienced a period of peace prior to the crusades largely because of the efforts of King Ladislas (1077-1095). Coloman, who succeeded to the throne, had the problem of controlling the crusading armies.

[6] The Count of Saint-Gilles was frequently used by Latin and Moslem writers to refer to the Count of Toulouse. Saint-Gilles was a thriving town at the mouth of the Rhone during the First Crusade.

[7] The Bishop of Le Puy refers to Adhémar. See n. 19 in preface.

I. The March Through Sclavonia and the Treachery of the Greeks

FOLLOWING ITS DEPARTURE, the army entered Sclavonia and underwent many privations during the winter season. Truly, Sclavonia is a forsaken land, both inaccessible and mountainous, where for three weeks we saw neither wild beasts nor birds. The barbarous and ignorant [8] natives would neither trade with us nor provide guides, but fled from their villages and strongholds and, as though they had been badly injured by our infirm stragglers, slew these poor souls—the debilitated, the old women and men, the poor, and the sick—as if they were slaughtering cattle. Because of the familiarity of the Slavs with the countryside, it was difficult for our heavily armed knights to give chase to these unarmed robbers through the midst of rugged mountains and very dense forests.[9] Yet our army endured these marauders because our soldiers could neither fight them in the open nor avoid skirmishes with them.

We break our story at this point to relate a glorious encounter of the Count which occurred one day along the route when Raymond and his band, upon finding themselves hedged in by the Slavs, rushed and captured some six of them.[10] The

[8] See our discussion of the date of departure of the Provençals in *Raymond IV, Count of Toulouse*, pp. 38-39. The forces of Raymond probably left during September and October, 1096. See Norman Golb, "New Light on the Persecution of French Jews at the Time of the First Crusade," *Proc. Amer. Acad. for Jewish Research* 34 (1966): pp. 1-63. Golb throws light on Jewish persecution in southern France. We are inclined to think that the Provençals did not engage in movements similar to those in Germany. Jews occupied a much higher position in the Midi. Certainly, there must have been cases of sporadic outbreaks against them by the poorly controlled elements in the Provençal army. The descriptive terms, "barbarous and ignorant," were used in classical times. See Cicero, *Oration for A. Licinius Archias*, 8.

[9] The crusaders gave chase through "the midst of rugged mountains and very dense forests" to no avail. This is, no doubt, drawn from Saint Ambrose, "On Psalm 1," *Patrologiae cursus completus Series Latina* (217 v. Paris, 1844-1864) 14: c. 932-935 (hereafter cited as *MPL*).

[10] The phrase, the Count of Toulouse "rushed upon" the Slavs, is used frequently in classical Latin. See Caesar, *The Gallic War* I, 22. The entire account of Raymond's skirmish is one in which he is perilously situated with a few companions. He is able through quick judgment and prompt action to emerge safely.

16

Count, now sorely pressed by their menacing comrades, realized that he must break through to his army and so gave a command to snatch out the eyes of some of his captives, to cut off the feet of others, and to mangle the nose and hands of yet others and abandon them. Thus, he and his comrades fled to safety while the enemy was horror-stricken by the gruesome sight of their mutilated friends and paralyzed by grief. In such manner he was freed from the agony of death and this perilous place by God's goodness.

Actually, we find it difficult to report the bravery and judgment displayed by Raymond in Sclavonia.[11] For almost forty days we journeyed in this land at times encountering such clouds of fog we could almost touch these vapors and shove them in front of us with our bodies.[12] In the midst of these dangers the Count always protected his people by fighting in the rearguard and by being the last one to reach his quarters. Some might return to camp in the middle of the day or at sundown, but not Raymond, who frequently arrived at his tent in the middle of the night or at the cock's crow.[13]

We passed through Sclavonia without losses from starvation or open conflict largely through God's mercy, the hard work of the Count, and the counsel of Adhémar. This successful crossing of the barbarous lands leads us to believe that God wished His host of warriors to cross through Sclavonia in order that brutish, pagan men, by learning of the strength and long suffering of His soldiers, would at some time recover from their savageness or as unabsolved sinners be led to God's doom.

Upon our arrival at Scutari [14] after our strenuous passage across Sclavonia, the Count affirmed brotherhood [15] and be-

[11] The virtues of Raymond, "bravery and judgment," are among those outlined by Ambrose, *De Officiis Ministrorum* in *MPL* 16: c. 60-76.

[12] "Forty days" is used symbolically. The chaplain was well aware of its significance in Biblical literature.

[13] Raymond was the last to arrive in camp "at the cock's crow." See Mark 13: 35. *Gallicantu* in medieval service books might designate one of the canonical hours.

[14] Scutari was a medieval town, now known as Shkodër in Albania. The Provençals arrived in Scutari toward the end of January, 1097. The chaplain wrote of the slaughter of the poor in Sclavonia but states that no losses from hunger or open conflict were sustained.

[15] "Brotherhood" is frequently used by Raymond. See William Daly, "Christian Fraternity, the Crusaders, and the Security of Constantinople, 1097-1204: The Precarious Survival of an Ideal," *Mediaeval Studies* 22 (1960): pp. 43-91.

stowed many gifts upon the king of the Slavs so that the crusaders could buy in peace and look for the necessities of life.[16]
But this was only an illusion, for we sorely regretted our trust in
the sham peace when the Slavs took advantage of the occasion,
went berserk as was their custom, slew our people, and snatched
what they could from the unarmed. You may well believe we
prayed for a refuge and not for revenge; [17] but why should
we continue this dreary account of Sclavonia?

On our encampment at Durazzo [18] we were confident that
we were in our land, because we believed that Alexius [19] and
his followers were our Christian brothers and confederates.
But truly, with the savagery of lions they rushed upon peaceful
men who were oblivious of their need for self defense.[20] These
brigands, operating by night, slew our people in groves and
places far from camp and stole what they could from them.
While the Greeks acted thus without restraint, their leader,
John Comnenus,[21] promised peace; but during such a truce
they killed Pontius Rainaud and fatally wounded his brother,
Peter, two most noble princes.[22] We had a chance for vengeance,
but we renewed our march in preference to vindicating our
injustices. En route, we had letters concerning security and
brotherhood, and I may say of filiation, from the Emperor; [23]

[16] Runciman thinks that the Count of Toulouse bargained with Bodin, a
prince of the locality.

[17] It was a Christian virtue not to pray for revenge. Ambrose warns against
revenge. See De Officiis in MPL 16: c. 62.

[18] Durazzo was the old medieval town of Dyrrachium located along the Adri-
atic coast. It was held by the Greeks at the time of the First Crusade. The
crusaders arrived there in the early part of February. See Steven Runciman,
"The First Crusaders' Journey Across the Balkan Peninsula," Byzantion 19
(1949). We have in most cases used the dating of Hagenmeyer. In general dating
of the crusade is subject to error. See Hagenmeyer, Chronologie, Nos. 116, 117
(hereafter cited as H Chr).

[19] Alexius Comnenus was a Byzantine leader who seized the throne, made
himself emperor (Basileus), and ruled the eastern empire from 1081 to 1118.
See The Alexiad.

[20] The enemy rushed upon the Christians with the "savagery of lions." See
Liber II Machabaeorum 11: 11.

[21] John Comnenus, who was stationed at Durazzo, was the nephew of Alexius.
He had instructions from his uncle on the reception of the crusaders.

[22] Pontius Rainaud and his brother, Peter, were knights in the army of the
Provençals.

[23] The chaplain uses a phrase, "I may say," as a device to add more information. See Cicero, "For the Manilian Law," 4.

but these were empty words, for before and behind, to the right and to the left Turks, Kumans, Uzes, and the tenacious peoples —Pechenegs and Bulgars—were lying in wait for us.[24]

[24] The crusaders followed the Via Egnatia. The chaplain shows his resentment of the guarded reception. The Greeks, on the other hand, were aware of the looting of the Latins. Kuman refers to a Turkish tribe called Kipchaks; the Pechenegs were people of Turkish origin known as Patzinaks to the Byzantines; Uzes were Turkish people sometimes called Oghuz Turks; the word *tanaces* we have translated as "tenacious people."

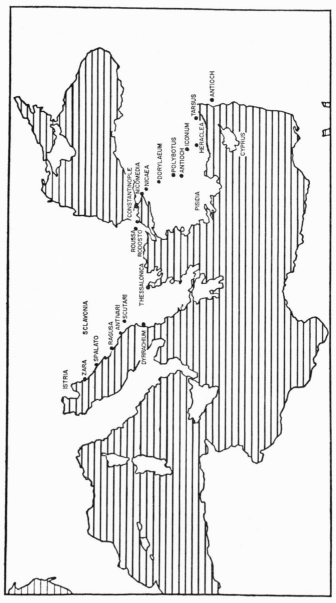

Map 1. The Provençal Route to Antioch.

II. The Journey Across Greek Lands and the Relations of Raymond of Saint-Gilles and Alexius

To ADD TO OUR TROUBLES, one day we were in the valley of Pelagonia when the Pechenegs captured the Bishop of Le Puy, who had wandered a short time from camp looking for a comfortable lodging.[1] They threw him from his mule, stripped him, and struck him heavily upon the head. But one of the fellow Pechenegs, while seeking gold from Adhémar, saved him from his fellow brigands; and so the great bishop, indispensable to God's justice, was spared to mankind because of God's compassion. When the commotion was heard in camp, the attacking crusaders saved the Bishop from the Pechenegs, who had been slow in dispatching him.

Thus, surrounded by treacherous imperial soldiers, we came to a fort, Bucinat, where Raymond heard that the Pechenegs lay in ambush for us in the defiles of a nearby mountain.[2] The Count reversed the tables by lying in ambush for them, and, along with his knights, took these mercenaries by surprise in a sudden attack, killing many and routing the others. In the midst of these events mollifying dispatches from Alexius arrived; yet still the enemy encircled us, and on all sides we were confronted with the Emperor's deceit.

Soon thereafter we arrived at Roussa, a town where the open contempt of its citizens so strained our customary forbearance that we seized arms, broke down the outer walls, captured great booty, and received the town in surrender.[3] We then left after we had raised our banner over the town and shouted *Tolosa*, the rallying cry of the Count. Our march took us thence to Rodosto, where mercenary troops of Alexius, anxious

---

[1] Pelagonia was an area located northwest of Macedonia. See Runciman, *op. cit.* (n. 18, chap. I) and *H Chr* 124, 125, 134 for the Provençal journey. The Provençals were in this area by the middle of February.

[2] Bucinat, the name of a castle, has not been identified.

[3] Roussa was a town in Thrace. Its Turkish name was Keshan. The attack on Roussa was made on April 12, 1097. See *H Chr* 118, 124, 125, and 134 for dates of journey from Durazzo to Constantinople.

to avenge the Roussa defeat, attacked us; but we slew a number of these hirelings and took some loot.[4]

Now our agents returned to us at Rodosto from the court of Alexius where we had sent them. They brought rosy reports of Byzantine promises largely because the Emperor bribed them; thus the following events need no further comment. Byzantine and crusader envoys urged Raymond to abandon his army and, unarmed with a few followers, to hurry to the court of the Basileus. They reported that Bohemond, the Duke of Lorraine, the Count of Flanders, and other princes besought Raymond to make a pact concerning the crusade with Alexius, who might take the Cross and become leader of God's army.[5] They added that Alexius was willing to transact all affairs beneficial to the trip with the Count in matters pertaining to him and to others. They further stated that the absence of such a great man's advice on the eve of combat would be unfortunate. Therefore, they pressed Raymond to come to Constantinople with a small force so that upon completion of arrangements with Alexius there would be no delay of the march. Raymond followed this advice, left a garrison in camp, and preceded the army on this mission, going alone and unarmed to Constantinople.

Thus far, the recording of these deeds, deeds marked by both a joyous and prosperous course, has been an agreeable task to the writer. However, the story is now pressed so with the burden of harshness and grief that it wearies me that I began what I have sworn to complete. Frankly, I do not know how to record these events in their importance. Shall I write of the most fraudulent and abominable treachery of the Emperor's

---

[4] Rodosto is the Turkish town of Tekirdagh located some four days journey from Constantinople. The Count of Toulouse met ambassadors from Alexius at Rodosto on April 18, 1097.

[5] Bohemond (1050ca.-1111) was the son of Robert Guiscard, who had fought the Greeks before the First Crusade. His father's patrimony went to a younger half brother, Roger Borsa. Consequently, Bohemond went crusading with the obvious hope of winning a state in the Near East. He did seize Antioch and was prince of that city from 1099 to 1111. The Duke of Lorraine refers to Godfrey (1060ca.-1100), who was a duke of Lower Lorraine. His role in the First Crusade was not brilliant although he did become Defender of the Holy Sepulchre. Later historians made him one of the great heroes of the movement. The Count of Flanders (d. 1111) sometimes called the "Jerusalemite" was the son of Robert the Frisian, who had made a pilgrimage to Jerusalem around 1087 to 1091. For biographies of these leaders see fn. 6 in preface.

counsel? Or shall I record the most infamous escape of our army and its unimaginable helplessness? Or by relating the deaths of such great princes, shall I leave a memorial of eternal grief? To the contrary, let whoever wishes to know inquire from others rather than from us.[6]

However, we shall report this very important occurrence. While all of our people dreamed of leaving camp, fleeing, forsaking their comrades, and giving up all which they had carried from far away lands, they were led back to such a steadfast strength through the saving Grace of repentance and fasting that only their former ignominy of desperation and desire for flight strongly embarrassed them. But we shall tarry no longer with this sad account.

Upon the most honorable reception of Raymond by Alexius and his princes, the Basileus demanded from the Count homage and an oath which the other princes had sworn to him. Raymond responded that he had not taken the Cross to pay allegiance to another lord or to be in the service of any other than the One for whom he had abandoned his native land and his paternal goods.[7] He would, however, entrust himself, his followers, and his effects to the Emperor if he would journey to Jerusalem with the army. But Alexius temporized by excusing himself from the march on the grounds that he was afraid that the Germans, Hungarians, Kumans, and other fierce people would plunder his empire if he undertook the march with the pilgrims.[8]

In the meantime the Count, after learning of the rout and death of his men, believed that he had been misled and through the services of some of our leaders summoned the Emperor on charges of betraying the crusaders. But Alexius replied that

[6] This passage reminds us of the later orators of the early Renaissance who used the device of leaving their audience without an answer to the questions which they proposed. Apparently, the chaplain was poorly informed at this point and resorted to this literary device.

[7] The Count of Toulouse was the subject of several reports on his religious zeal. He was reported to have stated that he would never return to his native land. We are certain that the stories reflect the current opinion of his character. The chaplain is spinning a pretty phrase at this point, probably based on what the Count would be expected to say.

[8] Raymond's use of "fierce people" following the word Kumans supports our theory that in a preceding passage (fn. 24, chap. I) he used Kuman and tanaces and in this chapter Kuman and *feras gentes*. Thus, we believe, that the *tanaces* were not a race but a general term for fierce people.

he himself had been unaware that our troops had plundered his kingdom and that his people had borne many wrongs, and that he knew of no legal grounds for the Count's investigation unless it was that while Raymond's army in its accustomed way was ravaging villages and walled towns his men fled at the sight of the imperial army. Yet he promised he would make amends to the Count, and he gave Bohemond as a hostage of his pledge. They came to judgment, and the Count, contrary to justice, was compelled to free his hostage.

Meanwhile, our army arrived in Constantinople and after it came the Bishop with his brother, whom he had left ill in Durazzo.[9] Alexius sent word again and again promising that he would reward the Count handsomely if he would pay the same homage as the other princes; but Raymond brooded over revenge for unjust treatment of himself and his men and sought means to remove the shame of such ill fame. However, the Duke of Lorraine and the Count of Flanders and other princes deplored such thoughts, saying that it was the height of folly for Christians to fight Christians when the Turks were near at hand. Bohemond, in fact, pledged his support to Alexius in case Raymond took action against him or if the Count longer excused himself from homage and an oath. At this juncture, following consultation with his Provençals, the Count swore that he would not, either through himself or through others, take away from the Emperor life and possessions. When he was cited concerning homage, he replied that he would not pay homage because of the peril to his rights. We may add that Alexius gave him little of worldly goods because of his intransigence.[10]

[9] The role of Adhémar in the quarrel of Raymond and Alexius is unknown. However, his admirers have his good counsel prevailing. See *Raymond IV, Count of Toulouse*, pp. 50-51.

[10] We have translated Raymond's oath to read that he would "not take away from the Emperor life and possessions." Krey and others have Raymond not sullying the "life and honor" of Alexius. Similar oaths were taken in southern France, and the Latin "honorem" is better translated as possessions. Actually, the Count of Toulouse took an oath similar to those in his land and was in no sense a vassal of the Emperor. See our article, "The Convention of Alexius Comnenus and Raymond of Saint-Gilles," *Amer. Hist. Rev.* **58** (1953): pp. 322-327.

III. The Siege of Nicaea and the Passage of Romania

THEN AFTER PASSAGE of the sea we hastened to Nicaea, where Godfrey, Bohemond, and other leaders, who were in the vanguard, besieged Nicaea, a city well protected by natural terrain and clever defenses.[1] Its natural fortifications consisted of a great lake lapping at its walls and a ditch, brimful of runoff water from nearby streams, blocking entrance on three sides. Skillful men had enclosed Nicaea with such lofty walls that the city feared neither the attack of enemies nor the force of any machine. The ballistae of the nearby towers were so alternately faced that no one could move near them without peril, and if anyone wished to move forward, he could do no harm because he could easily be struck down from the top of a tower.[2]

In short, as we have so said, Bohemond besieged the town from the north, the Duke and the Germans from the east, the Count and the Bishop of Le Puy from the south; and for the record the Count of Normandy was absent.[3] At this time we must record the following event. While the Count of Toulouse wished to encamp there, the Turks marched down from the mountains in two bodies and fell upon our army. Doubtless they had made their plans with the hope that while one contingent fought Godfrey and the Germans encamped to the east, the other group of Turks would enter Nicaea through the

[1] Nicaea was built by Antigonus around 316 B.C. and was located in Bithynia on Lake Ascanius. At the time of the crusade it was held by the Selchükids and governed by Kilij Arslan. The Count of Toulouse remained in the vicinity of Constantinople until May 10, 1097, and then departed for Nicaea. It is possible that his relations with Alexius were more cordial than Raymond d'Aguilers leads us to believe. See *H Chr* 148.

[2] Ballistae were machines of war often made in the form of crossbows and used to hurl missiles.

[3] The Count of Normandy (1054 ca.-1134) was better known as Robert Curthose, the Duke of Normandy. He was the son of William the Conqueror (d. 1087), who had gained the throne of England. Robert mortgaged his lands to his brother, King William II (Rufus), to go crusading. His military feats on the crusade were heralded by his contemporaries, but in all he was a rather obscure person in the political affairs of the movement. See C. W. David, *Robert Curthose, Duke of Normandy* (Cambridge, 1920).

south gate and go out another gate and thereby easily rout our unsuspecting forces. But God, the customary scourge of wicked counsel, ruined their schemes so that it seems that he planned the battle according to the following outcome. God caused the Count, who at the moment was about to make camp with his men, to attack that body of Turks which at the very same time was on the point of entering Nicaea. In the first charge Raymond routed and killed many of the Turks and then chased the remaining ones to a nearby mountain, while at the same time the Turks who had planned to rush the Germans were likewise put to flight and crushed.

Following this success, we built machines and stormed the wall, all to no purpose. The wall was almost impregnable, and the courageous defense with arrows and machines was frustrating. Finally, after five weeks of fruitless siege, through God's will some troops of the entourage of Adhémar and Raymond after a skirmish pushed forward at great peril to the foot of a tower. Under the protection of a testudo they sapped, undermined, and toppled it to the ground. The coming of night prevented the capture of Nicaea. By the next morning our efforts proved futile, because under the cover of darkness the defenders had restored the walls. Nicaea, gripped by fear, surrendered in great part because Greek ships which had been drawn overland now floated on the lake. Consequently, the Turks, isolated from their friends by this act, bowed to Alexius as they no longer hoped for help while they daily watched the Frankish army grow, a fact accented even more by the arrival of the Count of Normandy.[4]

Alexius had pledged to the princes and the Frankish people that he would hand over to them all of the gold, silver, horses, and effects of all kinds which were in Nicaea; and he further stated that he would found there a Latin monastery and hospice for needy Franks. He also promised to give so much to every person in the army that every soldier would wish to serve him at all times. The Franks trusted these sincere words and praised the surrender. But once in possession of Nicaea, Alexius acted

---

[4] Raymond's account of the siege of Nicaea is rather close to that of the *Gesta*, but there are details in each which indicate additional sources of information. The garrison surrendered to the Byzantine leader, Butumites, probably on the night of June 18, 1097. By the morning of June 19 Byzantine banners flew over Nicaea, *H Chr* 159, 160.

as such an ingrate to the army that as long as he might live people would ever revile him and call him traitor.

At this time we learned that when Peter the Hermit and his peasant hordes had arrived in Constantinople months before the main crusading force, Alexius had betrayed him by forcing Peter and his followers, unfamiliar with both the locale and the art of war, to cross the Straits with no defense against the Turks.[5] So the Nicene Turks, sensing an easy kill, rapidly and easily butchered sixty thousand peasants and missed only the survivors who escaped their swords by taking refuge in a fortress. The victors, emboldened and made arrogant by their success, sent the captured weapons and crusaders to their noblemen and to Saracen leaders in distant places, and wrote throughout their lands that the Franks were unwarlike.

Following these events, we left Nicaea bound for Romania; and on the march the next day Bohemond and some of the princes indiscreetly parted from the Count, the Bishop, and the Duke.[6] On the third day of Bohemond's diversionary march, as he was considering making camp, his soldiers beheld one hundred and fifty thousand men approaching in battle formation.[7] While he formed his battle ranks according to circumstance and made ready for the fight, he lost many stragglers; and so as the skirmish heightened Bohemond summoned to his aid the Count and the Duke, who were only two miles distant. The help was not slow in coming. The crusaders donned their armor, mounted their steeds, and galloped off to fight the enemy shortly after Bohemond's messenger brought the news.

The sight of the onrushing knights chilled the hopes of Kilij Arslan, the attacking leader, and he fled precipitately.[8]

[5] Peter the Hermit was an unknown person until Urban's call at Clermont. An ardent preacher, Peter stirred the peasants to start the ill fated marches to Jerusalem. Heinrich Hagenmeyer in his book, *Peter der Eremite,* has divested the Hermit of his legendary role in the First Crusade. However, Peter remained a popular figure with the chroniclers and represented to them an unselfish man of God. The reader will note that Raymond d'Aguilers uses every opportunity to show his hatred of the Greeks.

[6] Romania was loosely applied by writers and in this case refers to Anatolia.

[7] The reader cannot trust Raymond's figures. See Runciman, *The First Crusade,* pp. 336-341.

[8] The chaplain describes the battle of Dorylaeum (near the modern Eskishehir). The battle was fought on July 1, 1097, *H Chr* 169, and resulted in the rout of the Turks. Raymond does not report the diversionary attack of Adhémar of

It seems to us that it was poetic justice that Kĭlĭj Arslan, who had seized captives and many tents from Bohemond, now through God's power abandoned his goods. Although we did not see it, some recounted a remarkable miracle in which two handsome knights in flashing armor, riding before our soldiers and seemingly invulnerable to the thrusts of Turkish lances, menaced the enemy so that they could not fight.[9] Although we learned this from apostate Turks now in our ranks, we can certify from evidence that for two days on the march we saw dead riders and dead horses.

Following the defeat and repulsion of the Turks, we rapidly crossed through Romania in peace although an illness of Raymond retarded the march a bit.[10] Distasteful as the following may be to scoffers, it should be made a matter of public record because it is an account of the miracle working of divine mercy. A Saxon count in our army, claiming to be a legate of Saint Gilles, said that he had been urged two times to command the Count: "Relax, you will not die of this infirmity because I have secured a respite for you from God and I shall always be at hand." [11] Although the Count was most credulous, he was so weakened by the malady that when he was taken from his bed and placed upon the ground, he scarcely had a breath of life. So the Bishop of Orange read the office as if he

---

Le Puy and deals with celestial manifestations. Brundage emphasizes the military skill of Adhémar. Runciman thinks that it was the joint effort of the crusaders that won the day. Kĭlĭj Arslān was the son of Sulaimān and was known as Ibn-Sulaimān, and hence was called Solomon by the crusaders. Following the death of Malik-Shāh in 1092 he became ruler of Asia Minor and held weak control of it until his death in 1107. The divisive character of the Turkish states led to the success of the First Crusade.

[9] The author is careful throughout his work to offer details which can be corroborated by witnesses. This is apparently little more than style. The two knights in "flashing armor" are probably drawn from *Liber II Machabaeorum* 10: 29-31. Victory is brought through the might of the Lord, and heavenly protectors in shining armor slaughter the enemy. See Ambrose, *De Officiis, MPL* 16, c. 82.

[10] The chaplain omits all of the details of the burdensome march across the Taurus mountains. This lacuna is difficult to explain.

[11] The account of the illness of Raymond of Saint-Gilles suggests Isaiah 38: 1-6. The story of Hezekiah's restoration from mortal illness through divine intervention was well known. The Canticle of Hezekiah, Isaiah 38:10-20, is a part of the Office of the Dead. It is strange how the Count of Toulouse was deathly ill several times and then miraculously recovered to return to the field of battle within a few days. Hagenmeyer dates the illness of Raymond on August 5, 1097, *H Chr* 177.

were dead; but divine compassion, which had made him leader
of his army, immediately raised him from death and returned
him safe and sound.[12]

[12] The Bishop of Orange was named William and was an honored member of
the Provençal clergy. Following the death of Adhémar, William held the respect
of the crusaders until he died at Ma'arrat-an-Numān.

IV. The Investment and Early Siege of Antioch

THEREAFTER as we approached Antioch, many princes proposed that we postpone the siege, especially since winter was close and the army, already weakened by summer heat, was now dispersed throughout strongholds.[1] They further argued that the crusaders should wait for imperial forces as well as for reported reinforcements en route from France, and so advised us to go into winter quarters until spring. Raymond, along with other princes standing in opposition, made a counter proposal: "Through God's inspiration we have arrived, through His loving kindness we won the highly fortified city, Nicaea, and through His compassion, have victory and safety from the Turks as well as peace and harmony in our army; therefore, our affairs should be entrusted to Him. We ought not to fear kings or leaders of kings, and neither dread places nor times since the Lord has rescued us from many perils." [2] The counsel of the latter prevailed and we arrived and encamped nearby Antioch so that the defenders firing from the heights of their towers wounded both our men in their tents and our horses.

We now take this opportunity to describe Antioch and its terrain so that our readers who have not seen it may follow the encounters and attacks.[3] Nestled in the Lebanon mountains is a plain in width one day's journey and in length one and one-half day's journey. The plain is bounded by a marsh; to the east a river which flows around a portion of this plain, runs back to the edge of the mountains situated in the region to the south so that there is no crossing between the mountains and the river, and thence it winds its way to the nearby Mediter-

---

[1] Antioch was an ancient city which was situated on the southeastern bank of the Orontes River on a plain lying between the river and Mount Silpius. Its fortifications dated to the time of Justinian, and due to their repair by the Byzantines, the Selchükids, who had captured the city in 1085, stoutly defended the walls. The crusaders arrived before Antioch between October 20 and 22, 1097, *H Chr* 203.

[2] The chaplain has fabricated this speech from the scriptures; for example, "The Lord has rescued us from many perils," is drawn from II Corinthians 1:10.

[3] The description of Antioch follows the style of historians. See William of Tyre's description in the Babcock and Krey translation, pp. 200-204.

ranean. Antioch is so located in these straits made by the stream cutting through the above mentioned mountains that the western flow of the river past the lower wall forms the land between it and the city in the shape of an arrow. Actually the city, lying a bit to the east, rises high in that direction and within its enclosure embraces the tops of three mountains. The mountain situated to the north is so cut off from the others by a great cliff that only a most difficult approach is possible from one to another. The northern hill boasts a fortress and the middle hill another which in the Greek language is called Colax, but the third hill has only towers. Furthermore, this city extends two miles in length and is so protected with walls, towers, and breastworks that it may dread neither the attack of machine nor the assault of man even if all mankind gathered to besiege it.

In short, the Frankish army of one hundred thousand armed men encamped along a line to the north of the described Antioch was content to remain there without making a frontal assault. Despite the fact there were in the city only two thousand first-rate knights, four or five thousand ordinary knights, and ten thousand or more footmen, Antioch was safe from attack as long as the gates were guarded because a valley and marshes shielded the high walls.[4] Upon our arrival we took our positions helter-skelter, posted no watches, and acted so stupidly that the enemy, had they known, could have overrun any sector of our camp.

At this time regional castles and nearby cities fell to us largely because of fear of us and a desire to escape Turkish bondage. Our knights, ignoring public interest, left Antioch in the selfish hopes of acquiring some of these material benefits. Even those who stayed in camp enjoyed the high life so that they ate only the best cuts, rump and shoulders, scorned brisket, and thought nothing of grain and wine.

In these good times only watchmen along the walls reminded us of our enemies concealed within Antioch, but the Turks soon discovered that the Christians openly and unarmed laid waste villages and fields. Although I am poorly informed of the

[4] Raymond's figures are unreliable. See Runciman, *The First Crusade*, pp. 336-341. The designation of knights as first rate and ordinary means little to us. See R. C. Smail, *Crusading Warfare (1097-1193), A Contribution to Medieval Military History* (Cambridge, 1956).

Turkish movements, our foes shortly emerged from Antioch
or came from Aleppo, some two days journey away, and killed
our scattered and defenseless foragers.[5] These countermeasures
lessened our easy life, and the new opportunities for slaughter
and pillage encouraged the Saracens to patrol their roads more
consistently.

News of these events stirred the crusaders to pick Bohemond
to lead a counterattack. Although he could muster only one
hundred and fifty knights Bohemond, accompanied by the
counts of Flanders and Normandy and prompted by shame of
backing out of the venture, finally set out largely because of
God's admonition. They located, followed, and drove the
enemy to death in the Orontes. Then the Christians returned
happily with booty to the camp. At the same time Genoese
ships docked on the coast at Port Simeon some ten miles away.[6]
During this time the enemy gradually slipped out of Antioch,
killed squires and peasants who pastured their horses and cattle
across the river, and returned with plunder into the city.

We now pause in our narrative to describe the setting so as
to clarify coming events. Our tents stood close to the river and
a pontoon bridge, made of boats found there, spanned it.
Antioch also had a bridge at the lower western corner and a
hill opposite us upon which were two mosques and a chapel of
tombs. In returning to our account we note again that our
often outnumbered troops dared to tangle with the emboldened
opposition. But the Turks, often dispersed and routed, renewed
the fight partly because they were lightly armed with bows and
were very agile on horse back, and partly because they could
race back across their forementioned bridge. They also liked
to shower down arrows from their hill. I remind you that their
bridge was almost a mile from ours, and on the plain between
the bridges daily and incessant skirmishes took place. Because
of their encampment near the banks of the river, Raymond and
Adhémar bore the brunt of the raids. These hit and run attacks
cost the above leaders all of their horses because the Turks,

[5] Aleppo at the time of the First Crusade was governed by the shrewd Selchükid
leader, Ridvan, who played politics between the strong Shī'ite population and
the Fātimid faction.

[6] Port Simeon was a port town located at the mouth of the Orontes river.
The Genoese who landed there were allies of Raymond of Saint-Gilles. They
later assisted him in the siege of Jerusalem.

unskilled in the use of lances and swords, fought at a distance
with arrows and so were dangerous in pursuit or flight.

In the third month of the siege when the Count of Normandy
was absent, Godfrey ill, and prices sky-high, Bohemond and the
Count of Flanders were selected to conduct a foraging expedition into Hispania while Raymond and Adhémar garrisoned
the camp.[7] News of these developments caused the besieged to
renew their usual sallies. In turn, Raymond moved against
them in his customary way, put his footmen in battle order, and
then accompanied by a few knights gave chase to the Turks.
In the ensuing melee he captured and killed two of the assail-
ants on the hill's slope and drove the others across their bridge
into Antioch. The sight was too much for the footmen who
broke ranks, dropped their standards, and ran pell mell to the
bridge. In their false security, they threw rocks and other
missiles against the bridge defenders. The Turks regrouped
and made a counterattack by the way of the bridge and a lower
ford.

At this time our knights galloped toward our bridge in pursuit of a runaway horse made riderless by them. The footmen
mistook this to be a flight of the knights and fled in a hurry
from the Turkish charge. In the clash the Turks relentlessly
butchered the fugitives. The Frankish knights, who stopped to
fight, found themselves grabbed by the fleeing rabble, who
snatched their arms, the manes and tails of their horses, and
pulled them from their mounts. Other knights followed along
in the push out of a sense of mercy and regard for the safety
of their people. The Turks hurriedly and pitilessly chased and
massacred the living and robbed the dead. It was not disgraceful
enough for our men to throw down their weapons, to run away,
to forget all sense of shame; no, they even jumped into the
river to be hit by stones or arrows or to be drowned. Only the
strong and skillful swimmers crossed the river and came to
friendly quarters.

In the running fight from their bridge to our bridge, the
Turks killed up to fifteen knights and around twenty footmen.
The standard bearer of the Bishop of Le Puy and a noble
young man, Bernard of Béziers, lost their lives there, and

[7] Raymond uses Hispania to mean the land of the pagans.

Adhémar's standard was taken.[8] We hope that our account of
the shamelessness of our army will bring neither blame nor
anger of God's servants against us, because really God on the
one hand brought adulterous and pillaging crusaders to repentance and on the other cheered our army in Hispania.

Gossip of the flourishing affairs and a sensational victory of
Raymond's troops spread from our camp to Bohemond, and
as a result raised morale there. During an attack on a village
Bohemond heard a few of his peasants take to heel and yell for
help, and a force dispatched to investigate the disorder soon
saw a body of Turks and Arabs in hot pursuit. Among the
auxiliary group were the Count of Flanders and some Provençals, a name applied to all those from Burgundy, Auvergne,
Gascony, and Gothia. I call to your attention that all others
in our army are called Franks, but the enemy makes no distinc-
tion and uses Franks for all. But I must return to the story.[9]
The Count of Flanders rashly reined his horse against the Turks
rather than suffer the disgrace of withdrawing to report the
enemy's approach. The Turks, unfamiliar with the use of
swords in close battle, sought safety in flight, yet the Count of
Flanders did not lay down his sword until he had killed one
hundred of his foes.

As the Count of Flanders returned victoriously to Bohemond,
he discovered twelve thousand Turks approaching his rear
guard and he saw to his left a great number of footmen standing on a hill not far away. Following consultations with the
rest of his army, he returned with reinforcements and took the
offensive while Bohemond, with the other crusaders, trailed at
some distance and thus shielded the rear lines. The Turks have
a customary method of fighting, even when outnumbered, of
attempting to surround their enemies; so in this encounter they
did likewise, but the good judgment of Bohemond forestalled
their tricks.

[8] Bernard of Béziers was in the entourage of Raymond of Saint-Gilles. His
name appears as a witness in a grant of the Count of Toulouse to the abbey of
Saint Victor of Marseilles in 1094. See *HGL* **5**: p. 732. One standard bearer
of Adhémar was named Heraclius. See *HGL* **3**: p. 516.

[9] Raymond's broad use of the word Provençal confuses modern scholars.
However, Fulcher wrote of "Raymond, Count of the Provençals, with Goths and
Gascons." See McGinty, *op. cit.*, p. 22. The reader should understand that
Raymond is applying Provençal to all of southern France rather than to
Provence.

The Turkish and Arabic attackers of the Count of Flanders
fled when they realized the ensuing fight would be waged hand
to hand with swords rather than at a distance with arrows. The
Count of Flanders then pursued the foe for two miles and the
living could see the slain lying all along the way like sheaves of
grain in the field at harvest time. During this encounter Bohemond struck the ambushing forces, scattered, and routed them,
but could not prevent the previously mentioned mob of enemy
footmen from sneaking away through places impassable on
horseback.

I daresay, if I were not modest, I would rate this battle before
the Maccabean war, because Maccabeus with three thousand
struck down forty-eight thousand of his foes while here four
hundred knights routed sixty thousand pagans. But we neither
disparage the courage of Maccabeus nor boast of the bravery
of our knights; however, we proclaim God, once wonderful to
Maccabeus, was even more so to our army.[10]

Our response to the attacker's flight was such a diminution
of bravery that the crusaders failed to follow the fleeing Turks.
Our victorious army consequently came back to camp without
provisions, and the ensuing famine drove prices so high that two
solidi scarcely had purchasing power equal to one day's bread
rations for one man, and other things were equally high. The
poor along with the wealthy, who wished to save their goods,
deserted the siege, and those who remained because of spiritual
strength, endured the sight of their horses wasting away from
starvation. Straw was scarce and seven or eight solidi did not
buy an adequate amount of grain for one night's provender
for one horse.

To add to our misfortunes, Bohemond, now famous for his
brilliant service in Hispania, threatened to depart, adding that
honor had brought him to his decision because he saw his men
and horses dying from hunger; moreover, he stated that he was
a man of limited means whose personal wealth was inadequate
for a protracted siege. We learned afterward that he made these
statements because ambition drove him to covet Antioch.

[10] The chaplain shows his respect for the valor of Maccabaeus but wishes his
Christian soldiers to excel him. This is an example of the untrustworthy figures
offered by Raymond. See the *Breviarium Romanum* (hereafter cited *Breviarium*),
Dominica I Octobris, in *II Nocturno, Ex Libro Officiorum Sancti Ambrosii
Episcopi*, Lib. 1, 40. The author is probably repeating his breviary for this
passage.

In the meantime there was an earth tremor on the Kalends of January and we also saw a very miraculous sign in the sky.[11] On the night's first watch a red sky in the north made it appear as if the sun rose on a new day. Although God had so scourged his army in order that we might turn to the light which arose in the darkness, yet the minds of certain ones were so dense and headstrong that they were recalled from neither riotous living nor plundering. Then Adhémar urged the people to fast three days, to pray, to give alms, and to form a procession; he further ordered the priests to celebrate masses and the clerks to repeat psalms. Thus the blessed Lord, mindful of his loving kindness, delayed His children's punishment lest it increase the pride of the pagans.

I turn now to one whom I had almost forgotten because he had been consigned to oblivion. This man, Taticius, accompanied our army in place of Alexius; he had a disfigured nose and lacked any redeeming qualities.[12] Daily, Taticius quietly admonished the princes to retire to nearby fortresses and drive out the besieged with numerous sallies and ambushes. But when all these things were disclosed to the Count, who had been ill from the day of his forced flight near the bridge, he convened his princes and the Bishop of Le Puy. Then at the conclusion of the council Raymond distributed five hundred marks to the group on the terms that, if anyone of the knights lost his horse, it would be replaced from the five hundred marks and other funds which had been granted to the brotherhood.[18]

This agreement of the brotherhood was very useful at that time because the poor people of the army, who wished to cross to the other side of the river to forage, dreaded the ceaseless

[11] The writer's description of an earthquake was taken almost exactly from the breviary. See *Breviarium, Verna, Dominica Resurrectionis,* antiphon. It reads: "Et ecce, terraemotus factus est magnus"; Raymond reads: "Interea terremotus factus est magnus." Hagenmeyer dates the earthquake on December 30, 1097, *H Chr* 221.

[12] Taticius was the Byzantine commander who accompanied the crusaders to Antioch. The chaplain's dislike of him is rather strange in view of the fact that the Count of Toulouse was sympathetic with the Greek cause.

[13] We have in this passage a practical application of the idea of brotherhood. It is self-evident that the crusaders held councils and made decisions dictated by necessity. Apparently, the Count of Toulouse used his wealth to help the destitute. See Edmund Bishop, *Liturgica Historica* (Oxford, 1918) for an excellent discussion of the idea of confraternity. See Thomas N. Bisson, "The Military Origins of Medieval Representation," *Amer. Hist. Rev.* **71,** 4 (1966): pp. 1199-1218.

attack of the Turks; and few wished to fight them since the horses of the Provençals, scarcely numbering one hundred, were scrawny and feeble. I hasten to state that the same situation existed in the camp of Bohemond and other leaders.

Following the action of the brotherhood, our knights boldly attacked the enemy because those who had worthless and worn-out horses knew they could replace their lost steeds with better ones. Oh, yes! another fact may be added; all the princes with the exception of the Count offered Antioch to Bohemond in the event it was captured. So with this pact Bohemond and other princes took an oath they would not abandon the siege of Antioch for seven years unless it fell sooner.[14]

While these affairs were conducted in camp, an unconfirmed story spread that the army of the Emperor was approaching, an army composed, it was said, of many races, Slavs, Pechenegs, Kumans, and Turcopoles.[15] Turcopoles were so named because they were either reared with Turks or were the offspring of a Christian mother and of a Turkish father. They feared to associate with us because of their bad treatment of us along the journey. Actually Taticius, that disfigured one, anxious for an excuse to run away, not only fabricated the above lie but added to his sins with perjury and betrayal of friends by hastening away in flight after ceding to Bohemond two or three cities, Tursol, Mamistra, and Adana. Therefore, under the pretense of joining the army of Alexius, Taticius broke camp, abandoned his followers, and left with God's curse; by this dastardly act, he brought eternal shame to himself and his men.[16]

[14] This statement leads us to believe that Raymond confused his chronology. The *Gesta* has a similar story but places the date of the crusader's promise to give Antioch to Bohemond on the eve of the fall of the city. The surrender of Antioch to Bohemond, according to the *Gesta*, was contingent upon the failure of Alexius to reinforce the crusaders. See Yewdale, *op. cit,* pp. 60-61.

[15] The Turcopoles were used as cavalrymen by the Byzantines.

[16] The motives which led to the flight of Taticius are obscure. Anna Comnena indicates that Taticius was threatened by Bohemond. The *Gesta* wrote of his cowardice, and Albert of Aachen indicated that Taticius had planned to flee at the first opportunity. Raymond's explanation of the causes of the flight of the Byzantine leader is very weak, and there is no evidence that he ceded the towns of Adana, Mamistra, and Tursol to Bohemond. Apparently, the chaplain was poorly informed on the event and depended on rumors or other sources of information. Adana and Mamistra were towns in Cilicia and had been liberated from the Turks by Tancred. Tursol probably refers to Tarsus. See A. C. Krey, *The First Crusade,* p. 292. However, Raymond's spelling indicates that he refers to Tell Bashir (Turbessel). Taticius abandoned the siege toward the end of February, 1098, *H Chr* 230.

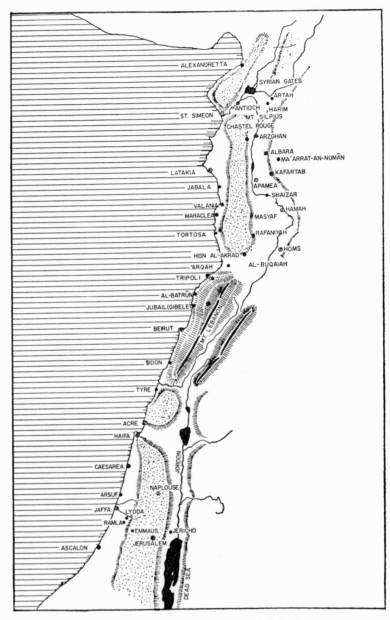

MAP 2. The Crusaders in Syria and Palestine.

V. The Later Siege of Antioch and the Tightening of the Blockade

NEWS NOW CAME that the commander of the caliph at the head of a large army from Corozan was bringing aid to Antioch.[1] Following a council of war in Adhémar's house, footmen were ordered to defend the camp and knights to ride out against the new force. This decision came because it was likely that the unfit and timid ones in the ranks of the footmen would show more cowardice than bravery if they saw a large force of Turks. The expeditionary group left under the cover of night and hid in some hills two leagues away from camp so that the defenders could not send word of their departure. Now I beseech those who have attempted to disparage our army in the past to hear this; indeed may they hear so that when they understand God's example of mercy on our behalf, they may hasten to give satisfaction with penitential wailing.

God increased the size of the six units of the knights so that each one seemed to grow from scarcely seven hundred men to more than two thousand. Certainly, it taxes me to know what to say of the bravado of the army whose knights actually sang warlike songs so joyously that they seemed to look upon the approaching battle as if it were a sport. It is to be observed here that the site of the coming fight was near the place where the river flowed within a mile of the marsh and thereby prohibited the Turkish customary encircling movements which depended upon the dispersion of their forces. Furthermore, God, who had offered the above mentioned advantages, now offered us six adjoining valleys by which our troops could move to battle; consequently, within one hour we had marched out and occupied the field. Thus as the sun shone brightly on our arms and bucklers, the battle began with our men at first gradually pushing forward while the Turks ran to and fro, shot their arrows, and slowly retreated.[2]

[1] Corozan has been identified as the Mosul area of Iraq. It was at one time the northern part of Iran which was designated as Khorassan. We believe that the chaplain uses the word to describe pagan lands. See Matthew 11:21. Raymond refers to Ridvan of Aleppo.

[2] Raymond's description of the battle is more dramatic than helpful. He does

39

Nevertheless, our troops suffered heavy losses until the first line of the Turks was driven against the rear echelons. Deserters later informed us that there were at least twenty-eight thousand Turkish cavalrymen in this encounter. When the hostile lines finally milled together, the Franks prayed to God and rushed forward. Without delay the ever present Lord "strong and mighty in battle" shielded His children and cast down the pagans.[3] Thereafter the Franks chased them almost ten miles from the battle site to their highly fortified fortress. Upon the sight of this debacle, the occupants of the castle burned it and took to flight.[4] This outcome caused joy and jubilation in the camp, because we considered the burning of the fortification as another victory.

At the same time fighting broke loose everywhere in the direction of Antioch because our foes planned a two-pronged attack—one from the besieged and one from the unexpected auxiliary troops. God showed no favorites and battled along with the footmen while he smiled upon the knights, so that the victory of the footmen over the besieged was no less than the knight's repulse of the reinforcements. With the battle and booty won, we carried the heads of the slain to camp and stuck them on posts as grim reminders of the plight of their Turkish allies and of future woes for the besieged. Now as we reflect upon it, we have concluded that this was God's command because the Turks had formerly disgraced us by fixing the point of the captured banner of the Blessed Mary in the ground. Thus God disposed that the sight of lifeless heads of friends supported by pointed sticks would ban further taunts from the defenders of Antioch.[5]

Ambassadors of the King of Babylon were present during these events, and upon viewing the miracles which God performed through His servants, praised Jesus, son of the Virgin

---

observe that the Turks could not make their encircling movements which had such deadly effect on the Christians. In this case the crusaders maneuvered the Turks into narrows near the lake of Antioch and the Orontes River.

[3] The ever present Lord "strong and mighty in battle" is borrowed from Psalm 23:8.

[4] Raymond refers to the capture of Hārim by the crusaders after the defeat of Ridvan. Hārim was east of Antioch.

[5] The author uses the idea of poetic justice when he has God willing the decapitation of the Turks and placing of their heads on stakes as punishment for their defilement of the banner of the Blessed Mary.

Mary, who through these wretched beggars trampled under foot the most powerful tyrants.[6] In addition, they promised friendship and favorable treatment, and reported benevolent acts of their king to Egyptian Christians and our pilgrims. Consequently, our envoys, charged with entering into a friendly pact, departed with them.

Contemporaneous with these events our princes decided to fortify an area on a hill which commanded the tents of Bohemond and thereby to thwart any and all possible enemy attacks against our tents. Upon completion of this work our fortifications were so strengthened that we were to all intents and purposes in an enclosed city made strong by work and natural terrain. Thus this new fortress, lying to our east, as well as the walls of Antioch and the nearby protecting marsh, guarded our camp and restricted attacks from the besieged to areas near the gates. Moreover, a river flowed to the west, and to the north an old wall wound its way down the mountain to the river. The plan of strengthening another fortification on the little mountain situated above the Turkish bridge also met with public approval, but siege machines which were built in camp proved useless.

In the fifth month of the investment at the time our ships carrying provisions docked in port, the besieged began to block the way to the sea and to kill supply crews.[7] At first the Turks threatened at all times largely because the indisposition of our leaders to retaliate emboldened them. To counter these dangers we finally decided to fortify the camp near the bridge. In view of the absence of many of our forces at the port, the Count and Bohemond were elected to guard the absentees' return as well as to carry back mattocks and other tools necessary for construction of the new fort. Upon learning of the mission of Raymond and Bohemond, the besieged began their usual attacks. In turn,

---

[6] King of Babylon refers to al-Afdal Shāhānshāh, vizir of Egypt. The Fātimids were willing to work with the Latins against their enemies the Turks. Alexius was sympathetic with the Fātimids and urged the Christians to cooperate with them. But the caliph suggested to the crusaders that Turkish Syria be divided between the Latins and the Fātimids. The proposal was rejected by the Latins who wished to take Palestine. See Sir Hamilton A. R. Gibb, "The Caliphate and the Arab States," *A History of the Crusades* 1 (1955): pp. 81-98.

[7] The proposed castle was located opposite the Bridge Gate. The fleet referred to by Raymond brought English and Italian pilgrims. Scholars are in disagreement on the question of the presence of Edgar Atheling.

our troops both unwary and disorderly advanced only to be shamefully scattered and routed.

When on the fourth day as the Count and Bohemond with a great multitude, secure as they thought in this rabble, returned from port, they were spied upon by the Turks. But why make a longer story of it? There was a fight, our troops fled, and we lost almost three hundred men and no one knows how much in spoils and arms. While we, like cattle in the mountains and crags, were being killed and dashed down, aid from the camp moved against the Turks, who then turned from the slaughter of the fugitives. Lord God, why these tribulations? Our forces within the camp and those without who had the services of the two greatest leaders in your army—Raymond and Bohemond— were overcome and vanquished. Shall we flee to the camp or shall the guardians of the camp flee to us? "Arise, Oh Lord. Help us in honor of your name." [8] If the report of the defeat of the princes had been heard in the camp, or if by chance we had learned of the rout of the army contingents, then collectively we would have fled. Now at the right moment the Lord aided us and incited those whom he had formerly cowed to be foremost in battle.

Upon viewing our stolen goods and his victory as well as the rashness of a few Christians, Yaghi Siyan,[9] commander of Antioch, sent his knights and footmen from the city. Confident of success, he commanded the gates of Antioch to be closed after them, thereby demanding his soldiers to win the fight or perish. In the meantime the crusaders, as ordered, moved forward gradually, but the Turks ran hither and thither, fired arrows, and boldly attacked our men. Our soldiers, unchecked by Turkish maneuvers, suffered but awaited the time for a mass assault. The flowing tears and plaintive prayers made one think that God's compassion must be in the offing.

---

[8] "Arise, Oh Lord. Help us in honor of your name," is frequently employed and used for effect. See the Ordinary as well as Psalm 34:2. Raymond's account of the ambush of the forces of the Count of Toulouse and Bohemond is very unsatisfactory. The chaplain is reluctant to describe it but uses it as a vehicle for his church lore. The mission of Raymond and Bohemond took place after a council which was held on March 5, 1098, *H Chr* 242. The ambush probably took place on March 6, 1098, *H Chr* 243.

[9] Yaghi-Siyan was the Selchükid governor of Antioch (1087-1098). The Turkish chiefs were unable to unite their forces, and the belated efforts of Ridvan, son of Tutush, did not succeed in relieving the siege of Antioch.

When the time for the encounter came, a very noble Provençal knight, Isoard of Ganges, accompanied by one hundred and fifty footmen, knelt, invoked the aid of God, and stirred his comrades to action by shouting, "Charge! Soldiers of Christ!" [10] Thereupon he hurled himself against the Turks, and as our troops rushed to the attack, the haughtiness of the enemy was shattered. The gate was closed, the bridge was strait, but the river was very broad.[11] What then? The panicky Turks were either smashed to the ground and slaughtered or crushed with stones in the river, for flight lay open to no one. Peace would have come to Antioch on this day had not Yaghi Siyan swung open the gate. I myself heard from many participants that they knocked twenty or more Turks into the river with bridge railings. There Godfrey distinguished himself greatly, for he blocked the Turks scrambling to enter the gate and forced them to break into two ranks as they ascended the steps.

Following a religious service, the happy victors marched back to camp with great spoils and many horses. Oh! How we wish you fellow Christians who follow us in your vows could have seen this noteworthy event! Namely, a horseman, fearful of death, hurriedly plunged into the deep waters of the river only to be grabbed by his fellow Turks, thrown from his horse, and drowned in the stream along with the mob which had seized him.[12] The hardships of the encounter were rewarded by the sight of the returning masses. Some running back and forth between the tents on Arabian horses were showing their new riches to their friends, and others, sporting two or three garments of silk, were praising God, the bestower of victory and gifts, and yet others, covered with three or four shields, were happily displaying these mementoes of their triumph. While they were able to convince us with these tokens and other booty

[10] "Eia" is very common in poetry and sequences. We have given a free translation because we think that "charge" expresses the meaning of the word in this passage. See *Salve Regina*. Isoard of Ganges is an obscure knight. He is not to be confused with Isoard of Die. The *C* manuscript writes of an Isoard of Gangia while others write of an Isoard of Gagia. *HGL* **3:** p. 511, attempts to identify this with Gaye or Gaiac, a place name in three areas of Languedoc, Razès, Lauragais, and Uzès. We think that Isoard was a knight of Ganges, a castle situated in the Cévennes (diocese of Maguelonne).

[11] Comments on the dangers of the broad way and the difficulties of the narrow way probably came from Matthew 7:13 or Luke 13:24.

[12] The author is happy to relate the drowning of the Turks. Deep waters are common symbols of misery. See Psalm 106:24.

of the greatness of their battle prowess, they could give no exact information on the number of dead because the Turkish rout ended at night, and consequently the heads of the fallen enemy had not been brought to camp.

However, on the following day at the site of a proposed fortification in front of their bridge, the bodies of some of our foes were discovered in a ditch close to a mountain which served as a Saracen cemetery. Excited by the sight of Turkish spoils, the poor violated all of the tombs and so, having disinterred the Turkish cadavers, there remained no doubt of the extent of the victory. The dead numbered around fifteen hundred, and I remain silent on both those buried in the city and those dragged under the waters of the river. But the corpses were hurled into the Orontes lest the intolerable stench interfere with construction of the fort.

Indeed, the sailors who in the flight of the Count and Bohemond had been routed and wounded were still terror stricken and skeptical of the outcome. But, as if strengthened by the sight of the great number of dead, they began to praise God, who is accustomed to chastening and cheering His children. So, by God's decree it happened that the Turks, who killed the food porters along the coast and river banks and left them to the beasts and birds, in turn made food in that place for the same beasts and birds.[13]

Following acknowledgment of victory and attendant festivities as well as completion of the fort, Antioch was besieged from the north and south. Then debate ensued over the choice of a prince as guardian of the new fort, since a community affair is often slighted because all believe it will be attended to by others.[14] While some of the princes, desirous of pay, solicited the vote of their peers for the office, the Count, contrary to the wishes of his entourage, grabbed control, partly in order to excuse himself from the accusation of sloth and avarice and

[13] We have another example of poetic justice. This time the dead Turks made food for the birds and the beasts which had previously feasted on Christians killed by Turks. See Jeremiah 16:4.

[14] The new fortification was called *La Mahomerie*. Gaston de Béarn, Peter of Castillon, Raymond of Turenne, William of Montpellier, Gouffier of Lastours, and William of Sabran helped the Count of Toulouse protect it. Stones from the Moslem cemetery were used to construct it, and work was probably completed by March 20, 1098.

partly to point the way of force and wisdom to the slothful.[15]

During the preceding summer Raymond had been weakened by a grave and long illness and consequently was so debilitated during the winter that it was reported he was disposed neither to fight nor to give. Although he had performed great services, he was considered an unimportant person because the people believed he was capable of more effort. He bore such enmity from the doubt cast upon his Christian strength that he was almost alienated from the Provençals. Meanwhile, the Count disregarded these insults, trusting that the besieged Antiochians, for the most part overcome, would flee; but, on the contrary, he was surrounded by his foes one morning at daybreak.

A great miracle of God's protection manifested itself when sixty of our men withstood the assault of seven thousand Saracens; and even more marvelous, on the preceding day a torrent of rain drenched the fresh earth and thus filled the fosse around the castle. As a result no obstacles but the strength of the Lord hindered the enemy. Yet I think that it is not the time to ignore the great courage of several knights, who as guards of the bridge, were now isolated and found themselves unable to flee since a distance of an arrow's flight lay between them and their fortress. Pushing forward against the Saracens in a circular formation, these knights advanced to the corner of a nearby house where they met courageously and intrepidly the enveloping attack, both the fury of the arrows and the cloud of rocks.

At the same time the noise of combat attracted our forces, and as a result the fort was saved from its attackers; however, despite the fact that the Turks gave up their drive at the sight of approaching reinforcements, those in the rear guard were destroyed although their bridge was close by. Again the ditch and the walls of the fortress were repaired so that the carriers of food could go and return safely from port. Consequently, the envy suffered by the Count calmed to the extent that he was called father and defender of our army, and following these events Raymond's reputation rose because single handed he had met the onslaughts of the enemy. After the blockade of the bridge and the bridge gate, the Turks made sorties from another gate located to the south and near the river. From here they

---

[15] Raymond of Saint-Gilles is used to display the chaplain's knowledge of the evils of sloth and avarice and the return to the way of force and wisdom. See *De Officiis, MPL* **16**: c. 137-138 for the consequences of avarice.

led their horses to a nook, which afforded an excellent pasture between the mountains and the river.

After reconnoitering and setting a time, some of our men circled around the city by crossing a rough mountain while others forded the river, and the combined party led away two thousand horses from the pasture. This number did not count mules and she mules which were retaken. It is to be noted that formerly many she mules en route from the sea to Antioch had been stolen by the Turks, and these animals now recovered were given back to their owners on proper identification.

Soon afterward Tancred fortified a monastery situated on the other side of the river, and in view of its importance in blockading the city the Count of Toulouse gave Tancred one hundred marks of silver, and other princes contributed according to their means. Thus it pleases me to note that, although we were fewer in numbers, God's grace made us much stronger than the enemy. At this time arriving couriers often reported enemy reinforcements; and, in fact, these rumors spread not only from Armenians and Greeks but also from residents of Antioch. I call to your attention that the Turks occupied Antioch fourteen years before and, in the absence of servants, had used Armenians and Greeks as such and had given wives to them. They, nevertheless, were disposed to flee to us with horses and arms as soon as escape was possible. Many timid crusaders along with the Armenian merchants took flight as rumors spread, but on the other hand able knights from various fortresses returned and also brought, adjusted, and repaired their arms. When the waning cowardice disappeared sufficiently, and boldness—sufficient at all times to brave all perils with and for brothers—returned, one of the besieged Turks confided in our princes that he would deliver Antioch to us.[16]

16 The crusaders fortified a castle where the old monastery of Saint George stood. A council of crusaders decided on April 5, 1098, to build the castle and they agreed to pay Tancred four hundred marks of silver to protect it. The Count of Toulouse contributed one fourth of this sum.

The author's reference to the Turk who confided in our princes has variants of this version. Manuscripts CDEFG agree with the A version and do not use "per Boamundum." The B manuscript does use "per Boamundum." B reads "quidem de Turcatis qui erat, per Boimundum in civitate, principibus mandavit nostris." This passage is not clear and leads us to believe that it is an interpolation.

VI. The Capture of Antioch

FOLLOWING a common council, the princes dispatched Bohemond and Godfrey as well as the Count of Flanders to test
this offer. Upon their arrival at a hill of Antioch in the middle
of the night, a messenger from the traitorous Turk commanded,
"Do not move until a lamp passes by." [1]

It was customary for three or four men carrying lamps to pass
along the walls, waking and cautioning sentinels. When the
lights passed, our men in the shadows of the wall set a ladder and
started to climb. A Frank, named Fulger and undoubtedly the
brother of Budellus of Chartres, fearlessly mounted the wall
and was followed closely by the Count of Flanders, who ordered
Bohemond and the Duke to follow.[2] However, in the hasty
ascent the ladder broke, but those who were already atop the
wall lowered themselves into the city and broke open a gate.
Entering by this means the crusaders killed all whom they met,
and at daybreak they cried out in such terrifying screams that
the whole city was thrown into confusion and women and children wept.

Some of the Christians in the nearby fort of Raymond,
awakened by the tumult repeated, "Enemy reinforcements
have come."

But others replied, "The cries of anguish are not the voices of
rejoicing."

Now as dawn broke our standards flew atop the southern hill
of Antioch. Panicked by the sight of our troops on the overhanging hill, some of the Antiochians rushed through the gates
while others leaped from the walls. The Lord threw them into
such chaos that not a single one stood and fought. After many
months of arduous siege this happy scene now unfolded for us,

---

[1] The traitor, Firūz, was apparently in the employment of Yaghī Siyan. He
was called Pirus, Pyrrhus, Firous, and Feirus as well as several other names.
The chaplain calls him a Turk. Other writers called him an Armenian. See
Runciman, *The First Crusade*, p. 231, n. 3. He was apparently disgruntled over
an unfortunate business transaction and an unfaithful wife. See *H Chr* 264
(June 2, 1098).

[2] Fulger and Budellus were obscure crusaders from Chartres.

a scene in which the long-time defenders of Antioch could neither escape from the city nor avoid death in daring flight.[3]

An agreeable and charming occurrence for us took place there when some Turks, attempting to escape unobserved through the crags separating the hill from the north, met a group of crusaders. Forced to retreat, the thwarted Turks spurred their steeds so hurriedly that all plunged together from the rocky cliffs. The fatal plunge of the Turks was indeed a pleasant spectacle for us, but we were saddened by the loss of more than three hundred horses dashed to death there.[4]

We shall not comment upon the amount of booty, but you may believe whatever comes to mind and compute more. We cannot estimate the number of slain Turks and Saracens, and it would be sadistic to relate the novel and varied means of death. In the meantime the defenders of the citadel, situated on a middle hill, observed the slaughter of their comrades and the cessation of the battle, and consequently chose to defend their fort. But Yaghî Sîyan, fleeing by way of one of the gates, was seized and decapitated by Armenian peasants, who in turn presented us with his head. Yaghî Sîyan, who had decapitated many Armenians, was, I think because of God's inexpressible will, in turn beheaded by their countrymen.

The city of Antioch fell on the third day of June, but it had been under attack from around October 22 of the preceding year. Our troops refrained from attacking the citadel while they examined and took inventory of the spoils; and further oblivious to God, the bestower of so many favors, they gormandized sumptuously and splendidly as they gave heed to dancing girls.

On the third day thereafter, being the fifth day of the same June, the crusaders were besieged by the pagans; and thus it happened that they, who had laid siege to Turkish Antioch through God's compassion, now found themselves hemmed in by the Turks through His will. To add to our fears the higher fortification, to all intents and purposes a citadel, was in their

---

[3] Raymond's description of the fall of Antioch reveals a certain sensitivity to the horrors of the attack and the plight of the Antiochians. He uses words from Psalms to intensify the action.

[4] The chaplain's joy over the death of the Turks and his concern over the loss of horses reveals the feelings of the newcomers, who had been conditioned to hate the Turks.

possession. Therefore, united by fear we laid siege to the fortress. But Kerbogha, lord of the Turks, shortly after his arrival, in the belief that the battle would be fought outside the city, made camp approximately two miles from Antioch and in orderly ranks advanced to the town's bridge.[5] On the first day our men bolstered the defense of the Count's fort, fearful that the occupants of the citadel might seize Antioch if the Christians marched out to fight. On the other hand they felt that, if they abandoned the fortress by the bridge, the enemy would capture it and block egress for fighting because it controlled exit from the city.

Roger of Barneville, a most illustrious and beloved knight, was following the retreating Turks one day when he was seized and beheaded.[6] Thereupon, sorrow and fear gripped our people, driving many to the desperation of flight.[7] Then in the ensuing encounters our foes suffered two setbacks, but on the third day they stormed the fort so forcefully that it seemed that only God's power protected it and halted the enemy, because for some unknown reason the Turks became panic stricken while in the act of crossing the moat and overthrowing the wall, and for that reason hurriedly ran away. Following a short withdrawal they saw no cause for flight other than their fright and therefore renewed the assault. They pressed forward furiously as if to wipe out their shameful rout, but once again were intimidated by God's power and consequently Kerbogha's men returned to their camp on the same day.

The crusaders burned the fort and withdrew into Antioch after their opponents returned the following day with heavy equipment. The anxiety of the Franks mounted while the enemies' confidence soared, because we had no hope outside the city and our foes held the key citadel within Antioch. These encouraging facts led the Turks to advance against us by way of the citadel; but the Christians, confident in their strategic positions and high ground, marched against the enemy and beat

[5] Kerbogha was the atabeg of Mosul. He made an error when he attacked Edessa en route to Antioch and thereby gave the Christians a chance to take the city.

[6] Roger of Barneville was the lord of Barneville-sur-Mer. The author of the *Gesta* mentions him in connection with the siege of Nicaea.

[7] "Sorrow and fear" are terms frequently found in Psalms. See Psalms 7:15; 12:2; 54:6.

them in the first attack.[8] Then, oblivious to a counterattack and preoccupied with spoils of battle, they suffered a disgraceful rout. At an entrance to Antioch more than one hundred Christians and a larger number of horses lost their lives; and as a result the Turks, upon entering the fortification, dreamed of attacking the city below.

A small valley, marked by a plain and water hole, lay between our mountain and their fort. Thereupon, the Turks strained with might and main to overrun and expel us from their route because descent into Antioch was possible only through our mountain. From morning until evening the fight raged with ferocity the like of which has never been reported. In the very middle of the hail of arrows and rocks, the uninterrupted clash of weapons, and numerous deaths, our troops fell into a deep sleep, certainly a most horrible and unusual experience for us. If you wish to know, the combat came to an end at night.[9]

Now at vigils, the time of trust in God's compassion, many gave up hope and hurriedly lowered themselves with ropes from the wall tops; and in the city soldiers, returning from the encounter, circulated widely a rumor that mass decapitation of the defenders was in store. To add weight to the terror, they too fled even as some urged the undecided to stand steadfast. Nevertheless, as we have said, God's pity was present even when Christians were troubled and sunk in despair, and in turn that which chastened His lascivious children likewise comforted them in adversity.[10]

[8] The citadel was occupied by Ahmad-ibn-Marwān, a lieutenant of Kerbogha's forces and a replacement of Yaghi-Siyan's son, Shams-ad-Daulah.

[9] The author knows very little of the details of this encounter and resorts to his usual devices. We have translated this passage to mean that the crusaders fell asleep. Unnatural drowsiness was not unusual in church lore. Raymond may have introduced this to explain the sleep of the soul, because he uses a vision in which the sinners must be brought back to the path of virtue. See Halldór Hermannson, "The Problem of Wineland," *Islandica* 25 (1936): p. 40. See also I Samuel 26:12 for "sopor Domini."

[10] Raymond refers to the rope dancers who deserted the siege of Antioch. They joined Stephen of Blois at Alexandretta and later hastened to inform Alexius of the plight of the crusaders.

VII. The Siege of Antioch by Kerbogha and the Finding of the Holy Lance

HERE BEGINS THE FINDING OF THE HOLY LANCE

FOLLOWING THE CAPTURE of Antioch, the Lord, unfolding His might and goodness, selected a Provençal peasant to console us and to deliver the following message to Raymond and Adhémar: [1]

"Andrew, the Apostle of God and our Lord, Jesus Christ, warned me some time ago on four different occasions and ordered me to report to you and, upon the fall of Antioch, return to you the Lance which pierced the side of our Saviour. Even today when I left with some others for the fight outside the walls of the city, I was trapped by two horsemen and almost crushed in the retreat. Dejected and listless I sank down upon a rock, whereupon Saint Andrew and a comrade appeared to me, a wretched sinner still staggering from affliction and fears, and warned me of added burdens if I did not hasten to deliver the Lance to you."

When the Count and the Bishop sought in detail the nature of the disclosures and the directives of Saint Andrew, the Provençal responded:

"During the Frankish investment of Antioch at the time of the first tremor of the earth, I was terror stricken and speechless

---

[1] The Provençal peasant was Peter Bartholomew. Raymond gives more attention to the story of the Holy Lance than do other writers. We have pointed out in our biography, *Raymond IV, Count of Toulouse*, p. 109, n. 3, that the author is elaborating on a briefer notice and is adding details necessary for a correct account of such a miracle. He weaves in events along with miracles to give the semblance of truth. We think that he is the creator of most of the account rather than a naive reporter. The whole story is sprinkled with words from Psalms—*Expecte, ecce, vigilasne,* and others. He does not hesitate to copy whole phrases to make his story move. For example, "Fair in form beyond the sons of men," is taken from Psalm 44:3; "Don't be afraid," is common; see Exodus 20:20. See Steven Runciman, "The Holy Lance Found at Antioch," *Analecta Bollandiana* **68** (1950). Peter supposedly reported the story on June 10, 1098, *H Chr* 277. The earthquake had taken place in period from December 30, 1097, to January 1, 1098.

except for 'God save me.' I was alone abed in my hut without the reassurance of friends; it was dark, and as I have said the shocks continued at length thereby adding to my anxiety. At this moment two men clad in brilliant garments appeared to me. The older one had red hair sprinkled with white, a broad and bushy white beard, black eyes and an agreeable countenance, and was of medium height; his younger companion was taller, and 'Fair in form beyond the sons of men.'

"The older man inquired, 'What are you doing?'

"I, all alone, was terrified and blurted out, 'Who are you?'

"Then he said; 'Stand up, do not be frightened, and listen to me. I am Andrew, the apostle. Arrange a meeting of the Bishop of Le Puy, the Count of Saint-Gilles, and Peter Raymond of Hautpoul [2] and ask them: Why doesn't Adhémar preach the word, exhort, and bless the people with the Cross which he carries daily? Certainly, it would be a great blessing to them.'

"And he further commanded: 'Follow me and I shall reveal to you the Lance of our Father, which you must give to the Count because God set it aside for him at birth.'

"Dressed in only a night shirt I got out of bed and followed him into Antioch to the church of the Blessed Apostle Peter by way of the north gate, in front of which the Saracens had constructed a mosque. Two lamps in the church brightened the interior as if it were midday. Then Saint Andrew told me, 'Remain here,' and further ordered me to stand by the column which was adjacent to the south steps leading up to the altar. While his companion remained some distance from the altar steps, Saint Andrew reached under ground, drew out the Lance, and placed it in my hands.

"Saint Andrew then spoke to me: 'Look upon the Lance which pierced Christ's side from which the world's deliverance arose.'

"As tears of joy streaked my cheeks, I grasped the Lance and

[2] Peter Raymond of Hautpoul (Alto-Pullo) was a vassal of the Count of Toulouse. The castle which bears his name was situated in the diocese of Lavaur, near the frontier of Narbonne and Carcassonne. Peter Raymond was active in the affairs of the siege of Antioch and died about the time of the passing of Adhémar. He was supposedly buried before the gate of the church of Saint Peter in Antioch. See *HGL* **3**: p. 517; **5**: p. 692; see also Tudebode, *Historia de Hierosolymitano itinere* in *RHC Occ* **3**: p. 33.

sobbed to Saint Andrew, 'Lord, if you so wish I shall take it from the church and put it into the hands of the Count.'

"And Saint Andrew replied: 'Wait until after the capture of Antioch, and then return with twelve men and search for the Lance in the same place where I revealed it and shall now conceal it.' And he buried it in the same spot. Following these revelations he conducted me over the city's walls to my hut and then vanished.

"Shortly, after reflecting upon my squalor and your eminence, I dared not come to you. Thereafter, following my departure to a fort near Edessa in search of food, on the first day of Lent at the cock's crow Saint Andrew in the same habit along with his former comrade came to me, and as a great light filled the house queried: 'Are you asleep?' [3]

"Awakened by his words, I answered: 'No, Lord, my sire, I am awake.'

"And he asked me: 'Have you delivered my recent message?'

"Then I replied: 'Sire, have I not beseeched you to send a more worthy one to them because, frightened by my wretched state, I have not dared to go before them?'

"Again he queried: 'Do you not know God's reason in leading you here, the greatness of His love for you, and His especial care in the choice of you? He ordered you here to vindicate scorn of Him as well as His chosen ones. His love for you is so great that the saints now resting in peace, aware of the favor of divine will, desired to return in the flesh and fight by your side. God has selected you from all mankind as grains of wheat are gathered from oats, because you stand out above all who have come before or shall come after you in merit and grace as the price of gold exceeds that of silver.'

"Following their departure I fell victim to a disease which so threatened my eyesight that I started ridding myself of my limited means, when I suddenly concluded that these ills beset me because of my disobedience of the apostle's orders, and thus reassured I went back to the siege. Reflecting again upon my wretched state, I said nothing because I feared that if I reported to you that you would cry out that I was a famished man who carried such a tale to secure food. Sometime later I was resting

[3] Edessa was an Armenian stronghold which was held by Baldwin, the brother of Godfrey.

with my Lord William Peter in a tent at the port of Saint-
Simeon on the eve of Palm Sunday when the Blessed Andrew
in the same garb of his past appearance and along with his
companion revealed himself to me and said: 'Why have you
not delivered my message to Raymond and Adhémar?' [4]

"And I replied: 'Lord! Have I not begged you to send a more
intelligent replacement, one whom they would heed; and besides you must know that the Turks kill anyone en route to
Antioch.'

"Then Saint Andrew countered: 'Don't be afraid; the Turks
will not hurt you. But tell the Count not to be dipped in the
River Jordan upon his arrival, but first row across in a boat;
and once on the other side be sprinkled while clad in a shirt
and linen breeches and thereafter keep his dried garments along
with the Holy Lance.' And my Lord William Peter can vouch
for the conversation although he did not see Saint Andrew. [5]

"Reassured I came back to the besiegers of Antioch, but I
could not assemble you as I wished, and so went to the port of
Mamistra. There while I waited impatiently to set sail for
supplies in Cyprus, Saint Andrew confronted me with grave
threats if I did not turn back to Antioch and repeat his instructions to you. [6] Then as I figured on ways that I could make the
three days journey from Mamistra to the crusading camp, I
began to cry hysterically because I realized that it was impossible. So finally at the insistence of my lord and comrades, we
embarked and for a whole day were pushed by oars and a favorable wind until sunset, when a sudden storm broke and drove
us back to Mamistra within an hour or two. Thus blocked
three times from passage to Cyprus, we went back to the port
of Saint-Simeon where I became very sick; but with the capture
of Antioch I came to you and now offer my testimony for your
approval."

The Bishop considered the story fraudulent, but the Count
immediately believed it and placed Peter Bartholomew in the
custody of his chaplain, Raymond.

[4] William Peter has been identified by Runciman as a pilgrim.

[5] The chaplain at a later time states that he does not understand why Peter
Bartholomew gave these instructions to the Count of Toulouse. He probably
added this information to make his story sound more truthful. See Ezechiel
44:17-19. These lines may have suggested Raymond's dress at the River Jordan.

[6] Cyprus was an important supply station for the crusaders and was apparently
well known to many of them.

On the following night our Lord, Jesus Christ, revealed himself to a priest, Stephen by name, who was crying as he awaited death for himself and his friends.[7] Stragglers from the fight at the citadel had terrified him by reporting a Turkish descent from the mountain and the flight and disorderly retreat of the crusaders. Before his approaching death Stephen, desirous of having God as a witness, entered the church of the Blessed Mary, confessed, received absolution for his sins, and began to chant hymns with his friends. He kept vigils while the others slept, repeating, "Lord, Who shall live in your dwelling? Who shall find rest on your Holy Mountain?" [8]

At this moment, a man, handsome beyond human form, appeared and asked Stephen, "Who has entered Antioch?"

Stephen replied, "Christians."

Then the man queried: "What do these Christians believe?"

The priest answered: "They believe Christ was born of the Virgin Mary and endured agony on the Cross, died, was buried, and rose from the grave on the third day and ascended to heaven."

Then the man inquired, "If they are Christians, why do they dread pagan hordes?" He continued, "Don't you recognize me?"

The priest, Stephen, answered, "I only know that you are most majestic."

Thereupon the man demanded, "Pay close attention to me."

As Stephen observed him closely, he saw appear gradually from above his head the form of a cross more dazzling than the sun. Then the priest replied to his interrogator, "Lord, we call images similar in appearance to you, those of Jesus Christ." [9]

The Lord continued, "You have spoken correctly because I am Jesus Christ. Is it not recorded that I am the Lord, mighty

[7] Stephen was at times called Stephen Valentine. He was probably a priest from Valence and was to figure in several visions.

[8] The chaplain has Stephen to repeat, "Who shall live in your dwelling? Who shall find rest on your Holy Mountain?" This is taken verbatim from Psalm 14:1. The whole vision of Stephen is a remarkable exercise in bringing the Scriptures to life. Raymond is very ingenious in this account.

[9] Raymond introduces descriptions of his celestial visitors which he must have drawn from current art. When he writes that "a man, handsome beyond human form," appeared we know that he refers to Christ and that even the most ignorant men knew this. See Saint Augustine, *De Civitate Dei, MPL* **41**: c. 548-550; also, Louis Réau, *Iconographie de l'art Chrétien* (Paris, 1955).

and powerful in battle? And who, may I ask, is your commander?"

Stephen replied, "Lord, we have no unified command, but we trust Adhémar more than others."

Then Christ commanded: "Tell the Bishop that these people by their evil deeds have alienated me, and because of this he should command, 'Turn from sin and I shall return to you.' [10] Later when they go to fight they shall say, 'Our enemies are gathered together and boast of their might; crush their might, Oh Lord! and rout them so that they shall know you, our God, alone battles with us.' [11] And add these instructions, 'My compassion shall be with you if you follow my commands for five days.' "

While he spoke thus a woman, Mary, Mother of Jesus Christ, whose countenance was haloed brilliantly, came near, looked toward the Lord and inquired, "What are you telling this man?"

And Christ answered Mary, "I asked who were the people within Antioch."

The Lady declared, "Oh My Master! They are Christians who are so often in my prayers to you."

When the priest aroused his nearby sleeping companion to witness the vision, Christ and Mary rose out of sight. The next morning, Stephen mounted the hill, *vis-à-vis* the Turkish fort, where our princes tarried with the exception of Godfrey, who guarded the mountain bastion to the north. In a called assembly Stephen reported the above vision, swore upon the Cross to verify it, and finally signified his willingness to cross through fire or throw himself from the heights of a tower if necessary to convince the unbelievers.

In view of the fact the masses believed that the princes now wished to escape to the port and only a few of them, steadfast in the faith, did not contemplate flight during the night past, the princes swore that they would neither flee nor abandon Antioch except by common council, and thus many were reassured. Even then only the closing of the gates of Antioch by

[10] The instructions, "Turn from sin and I shall return to you," are taken from *Prophetia Zachariae* 1:3.

[11] The crusaders were further instructed to say, "Our enemies are gathered together and boast of their might." This is a response; see *Breviarium Autumnalis, October*.

orders of Bohemond and Adhémar prevented wholesale evacuation; and despite all precautions William of Grand-Mesnil [12] along with his brother and many clerks and laymen deserted. Yet it happened to many who fled the city in the greatest peril to encounter a more perilous brush with death from Kerbogha's men.

Now reported revelations of our comrades became rife; and we too saw a wonder in the sky, namely a great star hanging over Antioch for a short time, then splitting three ways and falling into the Turkish camp. Somewhat strengthened the crusaders eagerly anticipated the fifth day proclaimed by the priest; and on that day twelve men and Peter Bartholomew collected the proper tools and began to dig in the church of the Blessed Peter, following the expulsion of all other Christians. The Bishop of Orange, Raymond d'Aguilers, author of this work, Raymond of Saint-Gilles, Pons of Balazun, and Farald of Thouars [13] were among the twelve.

We had been digging until evening when some gave up hope of unearthing the Lance. In the meantime after the Count had gone to guard the citadel, we persuaded fresh workers to replace the weary diggers and for a time they dug furiously. But the youthful Peter Bartholomew, seeing the exhaustion of our workers, stripped his outer garments and, clad only in a shirt and barefooted, dropped into the hole. He then begged us to pray to God to return His Lance to the crusaders so as to bring strength and victory to His people. Finally, prompted by His gracious compassion, the Lord showed us His Lance and I, Raymond, author of this book, kissed the point of the Lance as it barely protruded from the ground. I cannot relate the happiness and rejoicing which filled Antioch, but I can state that the Lance was uncovered on the eighteenth day before the Kalends of July (June 14).

On the following night the Blessed Andrew stood before the young revealer of the Lance and told him, "Behold God gave the Lance to the Count, in fact, had reserved it for him alone

---

[12] William of Grand-Mesnil was a brother-in-law of Bohemond. He was from Grand-Mesnil, a town south of Liege. William fled on the night of June 10-11, 1098, *H Chr* 278.

[13] Farald of Thouars came from Thouars, a town northwest of Poitiers. The *Gesta* related that thirteen dug for the Holy Lance. Raymond does not count Peter Bartholomew and prefers to use the number twelve, probably inspired by the twelve apostles. The Lance was found on June 14, 1098, *H Chr* 284.

throughout the ages, and also made him leader of the crusaders on the condition of his devotion to God."

When Peter Bartholomew sought mercy for the Christians, the Blessed Andrew answered, "Indeed the Lord will have pity on His people."

And again Peter sought from the nocturnal visitor the name of his companion: "Who was he whom he had seen so frequently accompanying him?"

The Blessed Andrew said, "Come close; kiss His foot."

Then the Provençal approached and saw what appeared to be a fresh and bloody wound on His foot, and as he held back because of the bloody sight, the Blessed Andrew commanded:

"Look upon the Father who was pierced for us on the Cross and has borne from that time forth this wound. In addition, the Lord orders you to celebrate the date of the discovery of His Lance on the octave of the following week, because the uncovering of the Lance at vespers prevents the celebration on that day; and thereafter on every anniversary of the day of the discovery of the Lance, you shall celebrate.

"Further, tell the Christians to restrain themselves as today's reading of the Epistle of my brother, Peter, teaches. (This epistle taught, 'Humble yourselves under the mighty hand of God').[14] Also the clerks shall chant daily the following hymn, 'Lustra sex qui jam peracta tempus implens corporis.' When they have chanted, 'Agnus in cruce levatus immolandus stipite,' they shall genuflect and conclude the hymn." [15]

Later when the Bishop of Orange and I inquired whether he knew the liturgy, Peter Bartholomew, under the impression that an affirmative "I know" would have brought disbelief, answered, "I do not know." Although he knew some ritual, he was so bewildered at the time that he neither recalled the liturgy nor had any recollection of what he had learned from it except the *Pater Noster, Credo in Deum, Magnificat,* and *Gloria in excelsis Deo,* and *Benedictus Dominus Deus Israel.* The others he had completely forgotten and only later could recall a few with difficulty.[16]

[14] The chaplain shows his familiarity with the Epistle of Peter, "Humble yourselves under the mighty hand of God," I Peter 5:6.

[15] We have chosen not to translate the hymn *Lustra Sex.* The hymn is the work of Venantius Fortunatus (530-609). The stanza beginning with *Lustra Sex* is used in part by the chaplain. We think that the Latin is preferable.

[16] Peter Bartholomew was ignorant because he could remember only part of the *Ordinary* and the *Gloria in excelsis* of Mass. This is a commentary on criteria for illiteracy.

VIII. The Rout of Kerbogha

D URING THIS TIME food became so scarce that a tongueless head of a horse sold for two or three solidi, a goat's intestines for five solidi, and a hen for eight or nine solidi. What can I report on bread prices when hunger remained after eating five solidi's worth? To those rich in gold, silver, and clothes it was neither unusual, nor burdensome to pay exorbitant costs. So prices were high because the sinful consciences of the knights lacked Christian courage. They gathered, cooked, and sold green figs, and also slowly boiled hides of cattle and horses as well as neglected edibles and sold them at such a high price that anyone could eat an amount costing two solidi. The majority of the knights, expecting God's compassion, refused to slaughter their horses, but did sustain themselves with their blood.

While these and other misfortunes too unpleasant to report beset the Christians, some of our men turned traitor and informed the Turks of the wretched state of Antioch and thereby added to our burdens. These reports stirred the Turks to bold and threatening acts, one of which occurred at noon one day. Around thirty of them mounted one of our towers, and for a time created panic; but our imperiled forces, fighting with God's aid, killed some of our foes and pushed others from the battlement. At this time all of the crusaders promised to follow the commands of Bohemond for a period of fifteen days after the fight so that he could arrange for the protection of Antioch and make battle plans. This decision was made because of the Turkish threat, the illness of Count Raymond and Adhémar, and the flight of Stephen of Blois.[1] I call to your attention that Stephen, despite the fact that he had been chosen crusading leader before the fall of Antioch, fled following rumors of the impending battle.

As we have reported, heavenly assistance came to our defeated, burdened, and distressed Christians through Peter Bartholomew, the finder of the Lance, who advised us as to our

[1] Stephen of Blois was a reluctant crusader. His wife, Adela, the daughter of William the Conqueror, urged him to take the Cross. His flight and subsequent disgrace was erased when he lost his life in 1102 in the ill-fated attack of Baldwin and his knights on the Egyptian forces at Ramla. See James A. Brundage, "An Errant Crusader: Stephen of Blois, "*Traditio* **16** (1960): pp. 380-395. Stephen left on June 2, 1098.

actions before and during battle. He told us that the Blessed Andrew commanded:

"All have displeased the Lord greatly and so have been afflicted; and you have prayed to the Lord and the Lord has hearkened to you. Now let everyone turn from sin to God and offer five alms because of the five wounds of the Lord; and if he is unable to do so let him repeat five times, *Pater Noster*. Following the completion of these commands, open the battle in the name of the Lord and let it be opened by day or night according to the princes' battle plans, because the Lord's hand will be with you. However, if anyone is doubtful of the outcome, open the gates and let him run to the Turks where he shall witness how Allah protects him. And further may any slacker who won't fight be with Judas, betrayer of Jesus Christ, who abandoned the apostles and sold the Lord to the Jews.

"In truth, let them go forth to battle with the faith of the Blessed Peter, holding fast to Christ's promise to him on His resurrection and appearance on the third day; and let them go forth to battle, because this land is not pagan but is under the jurisdiction of Saint Peter. Your rallying cry shall be, 'God aid us,' and, indeed, God shall aid you. All of your deceased comrades of the journey shall fight with you with the strength and leadership of God against nine tenths of the enemy, while you fight one tenth. Hurry into battle lest the Lord lead an equal number of Turks against you and blockade Antioch so long that you will eat one another. But rest assured that the days have come which Christ foretold to the Blessed Mary and to His apostles, the days in which He will hurl down and grind under foot the kingdom of the pagans, and in which He will lift up the Christian principality. But do not turn aside to the enemy tents for gold or silver."

Then the mighty hand of God so revealed itself that He, who ordered the above commands announced to us by Saint Andrew, strengthened all hearts with hope and faith so that each Christian felt that he had won a victory. Their zest for combat returned as they encouraged and exhorted one another, and the crowd, paralyzed by fear and poverty only a few days before, now questioned delay of battle and abused the princes.

Consequently, the chieftains set the battle date and then sent Peter the Hermit to Kerbogha, atabeg of Mosul, with orders that he abandon the siege of Antioch because it was under the jurisdiction of Saint Peter and the Christians. But the haughty Kerbogha answered that right or wrong he wished to become master of the city and the Franks, and he made the reluctant Peter the Hermit bow down before him.

At this time there arose the question of selecting some troops to guard Antioch from attacks from the citadel while others marched out to battle. So they made a stone wall and rampart on top of a hill facing the enemy, and fortified it with rocks, and garrisoned it with Raymond of Toulouse, who was seriously ill, and two hundred men. The day set for battle came, and that morning all took the sacrament, surrendered to God's will, even to death if He so wished, and to the honor of the Roman church and the Frankish race.

The battle order provided two double lines of Provençals from the troops of Raymond and Adhémar, with footmen in the van attacking or halting on command from their leaders, and the knights following as a rear guard. The same order of battle prevailed for the troops of Bohemond, Tancred, the Count of Normandy and the Franks, the Duke and the Burgundians. Heralds scurried through Antioch urging each man to fight with his leader. The order of the march was set as follows: Hugh the Great, the Count of Flanders, and the Count of Normandy first; then the Duke, the Bishop, and finally Bohemond.[2] In this manner they fell into their proper ranks below the city and before the Bridge Gate.

Oh! How blessed is the nation whose Lord is God and the people whom He has chosen for His own inheritance! Oh! How changing was the appearance of this army from sloth to activity![3] Only a few days before the leaders and nobles walked the streets of Antioch imploring God's help; and the commoners, crying and beating on their chests, went barefooted through the city. So dejected were the Christians that father and son,

[2] Hugh the Great was the son of Henry I of France and was known as the Count of Vermandois. He also went on the Crusade of 1101 and according to some accounts died at Tarsus as a result of an arrow wound.

[3] The description of the changed spirits of the Christians is opened by, "Oh! How blessed is the nation whose Lord is God." The author draws this from Psalm 32:12. It is also true that sloth is driven away by activity. Raymond does not hesitate to use his knowledge of proper procedure for Christians at such a moment. He also shows contrast by having Kerbogha troubled in soul as he plays chess.

brother and brother, exchanged neither salution nor glances as they passed on the streets. With the sudden change in spirit one could see the Christians go out as spirited horses, rattle their arms, wave their spears, and boisterously celebrate with acts and speeches. But why delay this story? The will to fight was now granted and the plans of the chieftains were executed.

In the meantime as Kerbogha played chess in his tent, he learned that the Franks were marching out to fight. Troubled in his soul at this unexpected move, he summoned Mirdalin, a Turkish refugee from Antioch and well-known courageous nobleman, and inquired, "What goes on? [4] Because the Franks were small in numbers did you not report the outnumbered Christians would never fight me?"

To this query Mirdalin answered, "No sire, I made no such report, but follow me and I shall observe them and advise you if you can overwhelm them easily."

As our third rank of crusaders advanced, Mirdalin scouted our ranks and told Kerbogha, "The Christians will die before they flee."

Kerbogha in turn inquired, "Can't some of the Christians be pushed back a little? "

Then Mirdalin answered, "If all the pagan world rushed against them, they would not budge a foot."

Despite his apprehension, Kerbogha formed his great army into battle order and permitted the crusaders to march out of Antioch unmolested, although he could have blocked them. Fearing encircling tactics from the rear, our forces turned their battle lines toward the mountains which were two full miles from the bridge. In typical clerical procession we advanced, and, may I add, it was a procession. Priests and many monks wearing white stoles walked before the ranks of our knights, chanting and praying for God's help and the protection of the saints. Nevertheless, the Turks attacked and shot arrows; but Kerbogha, no longer deaf to Christian proposals, suggested to

4 Mirdalin has not been identified. It may be a corruption based on Old French *amiral*, emir, from the Arabic. Wassāb-ibn-Mahmūd was an Arab officer who advised Kerbogha to attack the Christians as they came from the city. Kerbogha chose to attack all of them with the hope of winning a complete victory.

our leaders that five or ten Turks should fight the same number of Franks, and following the outcome the army represented by the conquered knights should leave the battle in peace.

Our men responded, "You refused when we wished this, but now that we are ready for battle let every man fight for his rights."

As stated, we were arrayed on the plain when a detachment of Turks to the rear of us attacked a contingent of footmen, who wheeled and met the attack courageously. The enemy troops, unable to budge the footmen, kindled a fire around them so that those undaunted by swords would be swept away by fire. Because of the extremely dry grass, there was a forced withdrawal.

Now with our army outside of Antioch, barefooted priests clad in priestly vestments stood upon the walls invoking God to protect His people, and by a Frankish victory bear witness to the covenant which He made holy with His blood. But in the advance from the bridge to the mountain we struggled mightily because of the encircling Turks, and in the course of this the enemy rushed upon those of us who were in Adhémar's ranks. Superior in numbers they neither wounded anyone nor shot arrows against us, no doubt, because of the protection of the Holy Lance. I was both a witness to these events and bearer of the Holy Lance. Furthermore, if the rumor is spread that Heraclius, standard bearer of the Bishop, was wounded in this melee, let it be known that he gave his standard to another and was far from our ranks.

With all of our soldiers outside Antioch our princes, as already stated, had formed eight lines; but five more appeared in our lines, thereby giving us thirteen ranks. Likewise, we shall not pass by this memorable event, one in which the Lord loosed a small but welcome shower as the Christians advanced into battle. Its drops brought to those touched by it such grace and strength that they disdained the enemy and charged forth as though nurtured in regal style. The shower affected our horses no less miraculously. In proof may I ask whose horse broke down before the fight's end although it had eaten nothing but bark and leaves of trees for eight days? Because God added soldiers to our army, we outnumbered the Turks in battle although previously we appeared outmanned.[5]

Upon completion of our advance and battle formation, the enemy fled without giving us an opportunity to fight, and our troops then chased them until sundown. The Lord labored surprisingly well with men and horses, for the men were not deterred by avarice, and those famished horses scarcely led from their scanty provender into battle by their masters, now pursued without difficulty the best and fleetest Turkish steeds. The Lord reserved this further pleasure for us; namely, the defenders of the citadel, upon viewing the flight of Kerbogha's men, despaired and some surrendered with the guarantee of their lives while others hastily took to flight. Despite this horrible and terrifying battle, few Turkish knights perished; on the other hand hardly a footman survived. In addition the booty included all of the Turkish tents, much gold and silver, many spoils, immeasurable amounts of grain, innumerable cattle, and camels. It brought to mind the flight of the Syrians at Samaria when a measure of flour and barley was bought for a shekel.[6] These events happened on the vigils of Saint Peter and Saint Paul, and appropriately so because through these saintly intercessors the Lord Jesus Christ brought this triumph to the pilgrim church of the Franks; indeed it was our merciful Lord who lives and dwells with his servants through all eternity. Amen.

[5] Raymond's description of the battle is not very informative. He prefers to write of processions of troops, comparing them with clerical processions. He uses the Holy Lance as a relic useful in battle, and he cannot resist having a sweet shower to fall on the Christians. Heraclius was a viscount of Polignac and younger brother of Pons. Polignac is close to Le Puy, and Pons and Heraclius had opposed the reforms of Adhémar.

[6] The victory of the crusaders brought to mind "the flight of the Syrians at Samaria." This analogy is drawn from *Liber Quartus Regum* 7: 18. The battle took place on June 28, 1098, *H Chr* 7, 309.

IX. The Death of Adhémar and Reports of the Visionaries

FOLLOWING THE VICTORY the Frankish leaders, Bohemond, the Count, the Duke, and the Count of Flanders, recaptured the citadel; but Bohemond, conceiving mischief by which he brought forth sin, seized the higher towers and forcibly ousted the followers of Godfrey, the Count of Flanders, and the Count of Saint-Gilles from the citadel with the excuse that he had sworn to the Turk who had delivered Antioch that only he would possess it.[1] Emboldened by this unpunished act, Bohemond came to demand the castle and gates of Antioch which Raymond, Adhémar, and Godfrey had protected from the time of Kerbogha's siege. With the exception of the Count all yielded. Despite his enfeebled state, Raymond did not wish to let go the bridge gate, and prayers, promises, and threats did not dissuade him.

Internal strife worried our leaders and further undermined friendly relations, so that only a few avoided disputes with their comrades or servants over theft or violence. In the absence of a judge who could or would discuss lawsuits, each person became a law unto himself. In these conditions the ailing Count and Bishop offered little protection to their followers. But why trifle with such petty details? Luxuriating in idleness and riches, the crusaders, contrary to God's commands, postponed the journey until the Kalends of November. We believe that, if the Franks had advanced, not one city between Antioch and Jerusalem would have thrown one rock at them so terrified and weakened at this time were the Saracen cities following the defeat of Kerbogha.[2]

---

[1] Ahmad ibn-Marwān, keeper of the citadel opened it to the crusaders after the defeat of Kerbogha. The garrison was permitted to march out, and Ahmad became apostate. Raymond indicates that the citadel was jointly possessed. The author of the *Gesta* states that Ahmad ibn-Marwān reversed his decision to surrender the citadel to Raymond and gave it to Bohemond. See *Gesta*, p. 158. Raymond states that Bohemond was "conceiving mischief by which he brought forth sin." See Psalm 7:15. The break between Bohemond and Raymond becomes very pronounced at this time.

[2] The chaplain reflects the usual misunderstanding of clerics when military

In the meantime Adhémar, Lord Bishop of Le Puy, beloved by God and mankind, flawless in the estimation of all, departed in peace to the Lord on the Kalends of August. So great was the sorrow of all Christians at the time of his passing that we, who had been eyewitnesses to it, could not describe the reactions when we turned to recording the greatness of events. The scattering of the leaders following Adhémar's death—Bohemond's return to Romania, and Godfrey's journey to Edessa—gave proof to his past usefulness to the *Militia Christi* and to its leaders.

On the second night following the Bishop's burial in the church of the Blessed Peter of Antioch, Lord Jesus, the Blessed Andrew, and Adhémar appeared in Raymond's chapel to Peter Bartholomew, the one who had related the location of the Lance in Antioch. Then Adhémar said to Peter:

"Thanks be to God, Bohemond, and all my brothers who freed me from hell. Following the uncovering of the Lance, I sinned deeply and so was drawn down to hell, whipped most severely, and as you can see my head and face were burned. My soul remained in hell from the hour it passed out of my body until my miserable corpse was returned to dust. This vestment you now see is one which the Lord returned to me in the burning flames, because at the time of my ordination as bishop I had given it to a pauper for God's work. Although Gehenna boiled up and the minions of Tartarus raved against me, they injured nothing beneath the garment. Of all things brought from my native land none brought as much benefit as a candle which my friends gave as an offering for me and the three denarii which I presented to the Lance. These benevolences revived me when, burning even unto death, I went forth from hell. My lord, Bohemond, said that he would carry my body to Jerusalem. For his sake he shall not move my corpse from its resting place because some of the blood of the Lord with whom I am now associated remains there.

"But if he doubts my statements, let him open my tomb and he shall see my burned head and face. I entrust my followers to my lord, the Count; let Raymond deal kindly with them so that God will be compassionate and carry out his

matters are involved. The delay at Antioch was dictated by problems of an exhausted army, supplies, and the season.

promises. Moreover, my brothers should not sorrow because of my death, because I shall be far more useful in death than in life if they are willing to keep the laws of God. I and all my departed brothers shall live with them, and I shall appear and offer better counsel than I did in life. You, my brothers, heed the burdensome and frightful pains of hell and serve God, the emancipator of man from these and other ills. Indeed, how fortunate is he who escapes the penalties of hell. The Saviour shall be able to bestow this pardon upon those who shall have kept his commandments. Also save the drippings of this candle left at dawn. Since I am dead let the Count and his chosen ones select a bishop in my place, since it is improper that the See of the Blessed Mary be without a bishop; and further give one of my cloaks to the church of Saint Andrew." [3]

Then the Blessed Andrew paid his respects, came nearer and commanded:

"Heed God's words which I speak. Raymond, remember the gift the Lord handed over to you, and that which you do, do in His name so that the Lord may guide your words and acts and grant your prayers. Nicaea, first city granted to you by the Lord, has been turned from Him. God gave His city to you, wrested it from your enemies, only to be denied in that place later because the works of the Lord were unknown there; and if one asked the Lord's help he was scourged. However, in His goodness the Lord does not wish to abandon you; and He shall grant that which you seek, and even more than you have dared to seek, because He delivered to you the Lance, which pierced His body from which ran the blood of our

[3] Adhémar died on August 1, 1098. The chaplain lauds him although he was angry with him because of his questioning of the Holy Lance. His account of Adhémar's return in a vision follows proper reporting. See a similar account in Saint Fursey's return in Benjamin Thorpe, editor and translator, *The Homilies of the Anglo-Saxon Church* (London, 1844-1846) 2: pp. 322-349. Adhémar was saved from punishment because he was a good man. See preface, n. 19, for pertinent articles on the subject of Adhémar's contributions. Brundage takes the position that we deprecate Adhémar's role. We state that the primary sources are very limited and that Adhémar's proponents have to argue *ex silentio*. We also argued *ex silentio*. In view of the fact that Adhémar died at a critical time, we cannot say that he could have held the crusaders together. Once the common danger was removed, it is not likely that Adhémar could have prevented the Norman Provençal split. The chaplain best expresses it when he has Adhémar say that he would "be far more useful in death than life."

redemption.[4] Remember the Lord did not give you this city to desecrate as you did the other, and you can certainly see that the Lord did not give it to you because of your merits.

"The Lord orders you, Oh! Raymond, that you learn who aspires most to rule Antioch and make inquiries concerning the Lord's role in his rule. Therefore, if you and your brothers, God's custodians of Antioch, find a faithful maintainer of God's justice, give him the city. But if he schemes to hold Antioch by force, thus scorning justice and judgment, then you and your brothers seek counsel from God, and He shall give it to you. Righteous men and the true worshipers of God will not fail you; but the unrighteous, may they return to him who is the enemy of justice, and it shall be seen in what manner God will save them. Truly, upon them shall be the same curse of God and His Mother as that which was placed on the falling Lucifer. If you are in accord, seek counsel in prayer, and God will give it to you.

"Further, if you are harmonious hold counsel concerning a patriarch of your law. Do not absolve captives wishing to keep your commandments, and do not admit those who have followed the Koran in order to worship Allah of the Turks.[5] Regard them as Turks and send two or three to prison, and they will identify others for you. Following completion of the above, ask the Lord's advice on the crusading journey and He will counsel you well. However, if you do not follow the above command, although Jerusalem is only ten days distance, you will not reach it in ten years; and I shall lead the infidels back into their lands and one hundred of them will triumph over you. Besides, you, servants of God, entreat the Lord as did the apostles; and as He answered their prayers so shall He answer yours.

"You, Raymond and Bohemond, go to the church of the Blessed Andrew, and he will give you God's best advice; and that which God places in your heart, follow it. After this visitation of the Blessed Andrew, not only humble yourself before him but

---

[4] The chaplain has a long account of Andrew's instructions to Raymond in which Andrew promises, "The Lord does not wish to abandon you, and He shall grant that which you seek." The phrases may be noted in Psalms 24:5-6; Deuteronomy 31.8.

[5] The author uses "Corrozanam" to represent paganisn, see n. 1, chap. V. See Matthew 11: 21; Luke 10: 13. We have taken the liberty of using Koran in view of the fact that the sense of Raymond's statement is made clear.

have your brothers to do likewise. By all means let peace and love of God abide with you, Raymond and Bohemond, because if you are in accord nothing can destroy you. It behooves you first to make known the justice which you must render. Let as many men as there are from each of their bishops declare publicly their wealth and assist their poor according to their ability and to the need. Further, act according to general agreement, and if they do not wish to observe this and other just rules, restrain them. If anyone desires to possess any city given to him by God for the Christians, may he conduct himself according to the above commands. But if he shall not do so, let the Count and the children of God scourge him."

At first credited, the admonitions of Saint Andrew were soon ignored, for some of the crusaders said, "Let us return Antioch to Alexius," but others objected.

Later at the siege of 'Arqah as Peter Bartholomew lay dying, he summoned the Count and instructed him: "Upon your arrival at Jerusalem command the army to pray God to lengthen and continue your life and God will double your life. Moreover, upon your return put the Lance within five leagues of the church of Saint Trophimus and have a church erected there; and upon oath make sound money there and do not permit any false acts in that place.[6] This spot shall be called Mount of Joy, and may these things be carried out in Provence because the Blessed Peter promised his disciple, Trophimus, to deliver the Holy Lance to him." [7]

The interests of the poor were set aside because of strife and dissension, and nothing happened concerning the counsel which the chieftains received from Saint Andrew. At this time the Turks from Aleppo invested a fortress which is called 'Azāz.[8] Troubled thus, the besieged Turks asked Godfrey, who was in the vicinity, to accept their castle because henceforth they preferred only a Frankish lord. Consequently, the Duke upon his return to Antioch called together Raymond, who had

[6] 'Arqah was a Moslem stronghold which lay some fifteen miles from Tripoli. The chaplain is anticipating events in his account and reveals his cleverness in writing history after the events.

[7] Trophimus was a legendary bishop of Arles and supposedly a disciple of St. Peter. See Acts 20:4 and 21:29. The instructions concerning his church are rooted in legend. The Mosque of the Prophet Samuel was called Montjoie.

[8] 'Azāz or Hazart was a mediaeval town located northeast of Antioch. The expedition to 'Azāz took place about September 14-17, 1098, H Chr 315.

recovered from his illness, and all his knights and footmen whom the Count had led into Hispania to pillage the countryside for the poor.

Godfrey also pleaded earnestly that Raymond, for God's sake as well as the honor of the Frankish race, hasten to help the apostate Turks, who now cried out to God; and he further stated that the besieged Turks made the sign of the Cross against the machines of the besiegers. Following these and other entreaties, the Count marched with Godfrey; however, the Turks abandoned the siege upon receipt of this news. Consequently, upon our army's arrival at 'Azāz, the Duke took hostages from the castle as guarantors of future loyalty, and Raymond returned to Antioch with considerable expense to his army. Here he called together his knights so that he could lead the poor people, now demoralized by hunger and weariness, into Hispania.

At the same time Saint Andrew appeared to Peter Bartholomew in a tent at Chastel-Rouge which was occupied by the Bishop of Apt, Raymond d'Aguilers, chaplain of the Count, and a chaplain named Simon. Simon, upon hearing the conversation of Saint Andrew and Peter, covered up his head, and, as he reported, heard much, but recalled only, "Lord, I say." [9]

However, the Bishop of Apt added, "I am not sure that I have dreamed or not, but an old man wearing a white stole and holding the Holy Lance of the Lord in his hands asked me, 'Do you believe this is the Lance of Jesus Christ?'

"Whereupon I responded, 'I believe, lord!'

"When he put the question a second and third time, I answered, 'Truly, I believe, lord that this is the Lance which drained the blood from the side of Jesus Christ by which all have been redeemed.' "

Then the Bishop of Apt shook me, Raymond d'Aguilers, as I lay sleeping close by. Upon awakening I noticed the extra light, and as if holy grace had entered my soul I inquired from my friends present whether they had felt as if they were in a group moved by great emotion, and all replied, "No, indeed."

While we repeated the above, Peter, the recipient of the

---

[9] Chastel Rouge was a crusader castle called Rugia. It was located south of Antioch. The Bishop of Apt was in the entourage of the Count of Toulouse. Apt was a town in Provence. Simon was a chaplain whose identity depends entirely upon the short notice of Raymond d'Aguilers.

heavenly revelation, answered, "Indeed you did see a pleasing light because the Father, author of all grace, stood in this spot for a long time."

When we requested him to relate the words of his heavenly visitors, Peter reported to us and the Count as follows:

"Tonight the Lord and the Blessed Andrew in their accustomed form came here accompanied by a small companion, wearing a long beard and clad in linen. Then the Blessed Andrew, displeased because I had abandoned the relics of his body, found in the church at Antioch, threatened me severely and continued: 'After being cast headfirst from a mountain by the unbelievers, I broke two fingers, and following my death this man preserved them and then translated them to Antioch. But you cared little for my relics after you found them; one you allowed to be stolen, the other you shamefully discarded.' Then he showed his hand which lacked two fingers."

Peter continued: "Oh! Count, Saint Andrew criticized you harshly because you are not afraid to sin grievously and evilly although you received the inexpressible gift reserved for you alone by the Lord. This is the reason the Lord gave you this sign: specifically, on the Feast of Saint Fidis five days ago you gave as an offering a candle large enough to burn three days and as many nights. Yet immediately melting, it sank to the ground. This night on the contrary you offered a small candle, one scarce large enough to burn until the cock's crow, and it sheds its light with only a third of the candle melted although it is now day.[10]

"Therefore, the Lord demands these things from you: 'Undertake nothing unless you have done penance, for if you fail to do so you and your undertakings will be as a melted candle which trickles to the earth. But God will make perfect and complete all your undertakings in the name of the Lord if you do penance, and the Lord will magnify even your small efforts as He has made the little candle, which you see, last a long time.' "

Raymond, although he denied the gravity of his sins, con-

[10] The story of the melted candle is rooted in the chaplain's knowledge of saintly lore. The longer a taper burns the greater the purity of the donor. When Raymond's candle burns briefly he awaits penance. See Patrick F. Moran, *Acta Sancti Brendani* (Dublin, 1872), pp. 107, 136. Saint Fidis Day was celebrated on October 6.

fessed and did penance after Peter Bartholomew confronted him with his sin.

Peter continued to address the Count: "Oh! Count, the Blessed Andrew objects to your advisers because they gave evil counsel for a purpose, and on account of this you are commanded to ignore their advice unless they swear not to give bad counsel knowingly to you.

"Listen well Raymond. The Lord orders you not to dilly-dally, because he will aid you only after the capture of Jerusalem; and let no crusader ride closer than two leagues when you approach Jerusalem. If you follow instructions God will deliver the city to you.

"Following these commands Saint Andrew thanked me profusely because I had brought about the consecration of the church which had been constructed in his name at Antioch; and he spoke not only of these things but of other matters not pertinent at this time. After this he and his comrades ascended into space."

X. The Capture of Albara and Ma'arrat-an-Nu'mān

SOON THEREAFTER Raymond, accompanied by the poor pilgrims and a few knights, marched into Syria where he courageously captured Albara, the first Saracen town on his route.[1] Here he slaughtered thousands, returned thousands more to be sold into slavery at Antioch, and freed those cowardly ones who surrendered before the fall of Albara. Thereafter, following the views of his chaplains and princes, the Count very commendably and properly selected a priest as bishop in this manner. One of the Count's chaplains, after a general convocation, climbed on the walls and made known to all the people Raymond's wishes. Because the people demanded an election, the above chaplain inquired whether there was a cleric who could receive the loyalty of the faithful, and by opposing the pagans as much as possible aid God and His brethren.

In the ensuing silence we called Peter, a native of Narbonne, and publicly made plain the burden of the bishopric, and urged that he take the post if he was determined to hold Albara even unto death. When he promised the above in his administration, the people unanimously approved him and thanked God very much in view of the fact they wanted a Roman bishop in the Eastern church.[2] Raymond gave Peter of Narbonne one-half of Albara and its environs.

The Kalends of November, the time for the reassembling of the crusaders and the renewal of the march, now drew near and Albara was two days journey from Antioch. As a result, Raymond left his army in Albara and journeyed to Antioch with Peter, his new bishop, many captives, and great booty. Here, all of the princes with the exception of Baldwin, brother of Godfrey, reassembled. This Baldwin, after digressing from the main crusading army, turned toward the Euphrates before

[1] Albara or al-Bārah was a town located southeast of Antioch. The expedition was made ca. September 25, 1098, *H Chr* 316.

[2] Peter of Narbonne was a priest in Raymond's army. He was consecrated by the Greek patriarch, John, as bishop of Albara, but as a Latin he incurred the enmity of the Greek clergy.

the capture of Antioch, seized the rich and celebrated city, Edessa, and waged many successful battles against the Turks.

Before going to other events I must tell you this tale. When Godfrey was on his way to Antioch with twelve knights, he encountered one hundred and fifty Turks, and, not the least hesitant, prepared his arms, exhorted his knights, and courageously charged the enemy. But the Moslems, impressed by the daredevil choice of death rather than safety in flight, chose to have some of their men dismount so that the mounted Turks would be assured that their dismounted friends would not desert them. As a result during the long and violent melee, Godfrey's knights, equal in number to the twelve apostles and secure in their belief the Duke was God's vicar, bravely charged the enemy. God gave the Duke such a great victory that he killed some thirty pagans, captured a like number, and pursuing the fugitives killed or caused to be drowned many others in the adjacent swamp and river. In a joyful triumph with the captive foes carrying the heads of their slain comrades, Godfrey returned victoriously to Antioch.[3]

Thereafter in a princely assembly in the church of the Blessed Peter, the princes began to plan the resumption of the march to Jerusalem. Then some of the holders of castles and rents in the environs of Antioch asked: "What shall be done about Antioch? Who will guard it? Alexius will not come; remember he fled when he heard Kerbogha besieged us, because he had no confidence in his strength or his huge army. Shall we await him longer? Certainly, he, who forced our brothers and those coming to God's aid to retreat, will not come to support us. On the other hand if we abandon Antioch and the Turks recover it, the result will be more disastrous than the last occupation. So let us give it to Bohemond, a wise man, respected by the pagans, a man who will protect it well."

But the Count and others spoke in opposition: "We swore upon the Cross of the Lord, the crown of thorns, and many

---

[3] The chaplain digresses a bit and mentions the work of Baldwin. See Fulcher of Chartres, I, XIV-XIX (ed. Hagenmeyer), pp. 209-243 for a full account. Harold S. Fink is working on a translation of Fulcher. The claims of Bohemond were presented by his followers. They based their opinions upon the fact that Bohemond was an able leader and would protect Antioch. The skirmish of Godfrey took place toward the end of October, 1098, *H Chr* 320. See William of Tyre VII, 4.

holy relics that we would not hold without the consent of the Emperor any city or castle in his dominion." [4]

Thus divided by contradictions, the princes became so violent that they almost took up arms. Actually, Godfrey and Robert of Flanders took the Antioch quarrel lightly and secretly favored Bohemond's possession, but fearful of the disgrace of perjury dared not commend it to him.[5] As a result the journey and all matters pertaining to it and the care of the poor were postponed.

The people, upon observing this princely fiasco, began to suggest first privately and later publicly: "It is obvious that our leaders because of cowardice or because of the oath to Alexius do not wish to lead us to Jerusalem; therefore, why can't we select a brave knight in whose loyal service we can be secure, and God willing we shall reach the Holy Sepulchre with him as our leader. My goodness! A year in the land of the pagans and the loss of two hundred thousand soldiers; isn't this enough? [6] Let those who covet the Emperor's gold or the Antiochian revenues possess them; but for us who left our homes for Christ, let us renew our march with Him as leader. May the coveters of Antioch die wickedly even as its inhabitants did recently. If the Antiochian quarrel continues, let us tear down the walls; then the era of princely good will existing prior to the city's capture, will return with its destruction. Otherwise, we should turn back to our lands before hunger and fatigue exhaust us."

Swayed by these and other views, Raymond and Bohemond made a peace of discord; and on a set date orders went out to the people to prepare for resumption of the crusade. Upon completion of all the details for this march, the counts of Saint-Gilles and Flanders along with the people on the set day marched into Syria where they besieged the wealthy and heavily populated city of Ma'arrat-an-Nu'mān, which was situated eight

---

[4] This passage reflects Raymond's respect for the oath which he had taken in Constantinople. The discussions took place in early November and the meeting in St. Peter's church took place on November 5, 1098, *H Chr* 321-323.

[5] Godfrey and Robert of Flanders reveal that they did not wish an open break with Alexius.

[6] The chaplain again presents the impractical views of the lower clergy and the pilgrims. See Walter Porges, "The Clergy, the Poor, and the Non-Combatants on the First Crusade," *Speculum* 21 (1946): pp. 21-23.

miles from Albara.[7] Because of a former skirmish with us in which we suffered heavy losses, the haughty citizens of the city railed at our leaders, cursed our army, and desecrated crosses fixed to their walls to anger us. On the day following our arrival, we were so angered by the natives that we openly stormed the walls and would, no doubt, have seized Ma'arrat-an-Nu'mān if we had possessed four more ladders. However, our two ladders, short and fragile, were mounted fearfully; and it was the council's decision to build machines, hurdles, and mounds by which the wall could be reached, sapped, and tumbled to the ground. While this went on Bohemond and his army came and laid siege to another sector of Ma'arrat-an-Nu'mān. As we stated above, we were inadequately prepared, but urged on by the newcomer's appearance we hoped to launch a new attack by filling the moat. But our new attack, more miserable than the first, was useless.

It grieves me to report that in the ensuing famine one could see more than ten thousand men scattered like cattle in the field scratching and looking, trying to find grains of wheat, barley, beans or any legume.[8] Despite the continuing work on assault machines, some of our people, impressed by the misery around them and the audacity of the Saracens, lost hope of God's mercy and turned tail.

But God, the protector of His servants, now had mercy on His people when he saw them in the slough of despond. As a result He employed the Blessed Apostles Peter and Andrew to inform us of His will and of ways to appease His harsh command. In the middle of the night they entered the Count's chapel and awakened Peter Bartholomew, the one to whom they had shown the Lance. But Peter Bartholomew, suddenly aroused, upon seeing two ugly and filthily clad characters standing by the reliquary, naturally believed them to be thieving paupers. Saint Andrew was clad in an old tunic, torn at the shoulders, the left one patched with cloth, the right one bare,

[7] Ma'arrat-an-Numān was located southeast of Albara and Antioch. The crusaders departed on November 23, besieged the town on November 28, and on the following day were assisted by Bohemond in a futile operation, *H Chr* 324, 325, 327.

[8] Raymond's description of gleaning in the fields is probably stylistic. However, Ralph of Caen, who disliked the Provençals, had jibed that the Provençals "lived on little, and were known to eat roots." See Radulphus Cadomensis, *Gesta Tancredi in expeditione Hierosolymitana, RHC Occ* (Paris) **3**: p. 651.

and he wore cheap shoes. Peter was dressed in an ankle-length, coarse linen shirt.

Then Peter Bartholomew inquired, "Who are you, my lords, and what do you seek?"

The Blessed Peter answered: "We are God's messengers; I am Peter and this is Andrew. But we chose this habit for our appearance so that you may observe the great profits for him who serves God devotedly. In this state and garb, just as you see us, we came to God, and behold us now."

After these remarks Peter and Andrew became brighter and more beautiful than words can express; and Peter Bartholomew, terror stricken by the unexpected flash of light, tumbled to the ground as if dead, and in his anxiety broke into a sweat which dampened the mat upon which he had fallen. Thereupon Saint Peter helped him to his feet and said, "You fell easily."

Peter Bartholomew replied, "Yes, my lord."

Saint Peter then explained, "So shall all disbelievers and transgressors of the Lord's command fall, but the Lord raises them as I did you after your fall if they repent their evil deeds and cry out to God. Furthermore, as your sweat remains on the mat, so surely God will lift up and remove the sins of those crying out to Him. But tell me, how does the army conduct itself?"

Peter Bartholomew answered, "Certainly, they are greatly worried by famine, and they are very miserable."

Whereupon Saint Peter stormed: "Deserters of Almighty God may well be fearful for having so forgotten the perils from which He delivered them that they failed to offer thanks. But you cried out to God when you were down and out at Antioch so that we in heaven might hear. The Lord heard you, offered you His Lance as a pledge of victory to you, and gave you a marvelous and glorious triumph over the besiegers and Kerbogha. You have deeply offended God; and now in what lord do you believe yourself to be safe? Can towering mountains or hidden caves protect you? You could not be safe even on some impregnable height stocked with all necessities, because one hundred thousand foes would menace each of you. In your ranks there is murder, pillage, and theft, as well as an absence of justice. There is also adultery, although it would be pleasing to God if you would marry. In the matters of justice the Lord orders that all goods in the dwelling of the violent oppressor of the poor shall be public property. If you pay your tithes the Lord is prepared to give you that which you need; but he will give Ma'arrat-an-Nu'mān to you on account of His mercy and not because of your deeds; and whenever you wish besiege it; do so because, without doubt, it will be seized."

Following Peter's account of these events next morning to the Count, Raymond along with the bishops of Orange and Albara called together the people; and, enticed by high hopes of capturing the city, the faithful gave generously and offered prayers to Almighty God to liberate His poor people for His name's sake only. Upon completion of these spiritual preparations, ladders were hastily made, a wooden tower erected, hurdles put together, and at the end of the day the assault was started. The besieged of Ma'arrat-an-Nu'mān hurled stones from catapults, darts, fire, hives of bees, and lime upon our men who had sapped their walls; but scarcely any suffered injury because of the power and mercy of God. On the other hand, the crusaders daringly attacked the walls with rocks and ladders in an assault lasting from sunrise until sunset; indeed it was a remarkable fight in that no one rested and no one doubted the victorious outcome. Finally all called out to God to be merciful to His people and to execute the promises of His disciples.

The ever present Lord delivered the city to us as His apostles had prophesied. Gouffier of Lastours, first to mount the walls, was followed by other Christians, who attacked the ramparts and towers; but night ended the fight and left some towers and parts of the town in Saracen hands.[9] The knights, anticipating a last ditch stand of the enemy the following morning, guarded the outer walls to cut off any escapees. But some crusaders, careless of their lives because starvation had made them contemptuous of life, carried the fight to the besieged in the shades of night. Thereby the poor gained the lion's share of booty and houses in Ma'arrat-an-Nu'mān while the knights, who awaited morning to enter, found poor pickings. In the meantime the pagans hid in subterranean caves, and practically none appeared on the streets. The Christians filched all the goods above the ground, and, driven by hopes of Saracen

[9] Gouffier of Lastours was lord of Lastours, near Nexon (Haute-Vienne). He was originally from Limousin. See *Notitiae duae Lemovicenses de praedicatione crucis in Aquitania, RHC Occ* (Paris, 1895) 5: p. 351. Ma'arrat-an-Numān fell on December 11, 1098, *H Chr* 329.

wealth underground, smoked the enemy out of their caves with fire and sulphur fumes. When the plunder in the caves proved disappointing, they tortured to death the hapless Moslems in their reach. Some of our men had the experience of leading the Saracens through the streets, hoping to locate spoils of war, only to find their captives would lead them to wells and then suddently jump headlong to their deaths in preference to revealing goods owned by them or others. Because of their intransigence all submitted to death. Their corpses were thrown into swamps and areas beyond the walls, and so Ma'arrat-an-Nu'mān yielded little plunder.[10]

The knights of Bohemond, although only half hearted in pressing the siege, acquired the greater number of towers, horses, and captives, and thereby led to hard feelings between the Normans and the Provençals. Now the Lord had brought to pass a miraculous event; and, as I reported above, even though we explained to the people before the capture of Ma'arrat-an-Nu'mān the apostolic commands of Peter and Andrew, Bohemond and his comrades ridiculed us. Actually Bohemond and his Normans were more of a hindrance than a help, and naturally the entourage of Raymond was indignant because the Normans held the major share of the spoils. Finally, the lords disagreed; Raymond wanted to give the city to the Bishop of Albara, and Bohemond held to some of his captured towers and warned, "I shall agree to nothing with Raymond unless he cedes the Antiochian towers to me."

In this turmoil knights and the people asked when it would please the princes to begin the journey, for although the march had started long ago, yet each day seemed to be the start of a new crusade for the goal had not been reached. Bohemond answered that he would not go before Easter, and it was now the time of the Nativity of our Lord. Many gave up hope and turned back on account of the scarcity of horses, the absence of Godfrey, and the exodus of many knights to Baldwin of Edessa.

At last, the Bishop of Albara and some nobles met with the poor people and called upon Raymond for help. When the Bishop ended his sermon, the knights and all the people knelt before the Count, the recipient of the Holy Lance, and tear-

[10] The reporting of the slaughter of the citizens of Ma'arrat-an-Numān is very descriptive and seems to be free of Biblical references.

fully beseeched him to make himself leader and lord of the army. They further stated that in view of the merits of his possession of the Holy Lance and the fact that he was beholden for the Lord's benefaction, he would not fear to continue the journey in safety with the people. Failing to do so Raymond should hand over the Lance to the masses, and they would continue the march to the Holy City under the Lord's leadership. The Count temporized, fearing that the absentee princes, already envious of him, would not follow him if he set the day of departure.

Why not end this dreary story? The tears of the poor prevailed, and Raymond set the departure date on the fifteenth day while the infuriated Bohemond proclaimed throughout the town the date of departure as the fifth or sixth day, and soon thereafter returned to Antioch. Raymond and the Bishop of Albara turned to providing a garrison, determining both the number and choice of personnel. At the same time the Count requested Godfrey and the absentees from Ma'arrat-an-Nu'mān to come together in one place and make the necessary preparation for resumption of the journey. The princes met and held a conference at Chastel-Rouge, which is almost halfway between Antioch and Ma'arrat-an-Nu'mān; but the meeting came to naught because the leaders and many who followed their example offered reasons for not continuing the journey. As a result Raymond offered Godfrey and Robert of Normandy ten thousand solidi apiece, six thousand to Robert of Flanders, five thousand to Tancred, and proportionately to others.[11]

[11] The preliminary negotiations of Bohemond and Raymond probably took place on December 29, 1098, with Raymond's date of departure set on January 13, 1099. The meeting at Chastel-Rouge took place probably on January 4, 1099. Following the failure of the conference to appease Bohemond, the Norman leader returned to Antioch. Runciman thinks that Raymond's offer to the leaders was a bribe. Grousset suggests that Raymond coveted Jerusalem at this time and wished to enlist aid from his fellow crusaders. We believe that the offer was accepted and that the differences in sums represent the merits of the leaders. Two types of money used by the Count of Toulouse are extant. One is the Melgorien which was coined by the counts of Melgueil. The other is the money of Saint-Gilles which some claim was that of Raymond V. A good horse cost two hundred Melgorien or about four marks (two pounds of silver). See Jean Pierre Papon, *Histoire générale de Provence* (Paris, 1778) **2**: pp. 538, 541, 551, 552; also, Mireille Castaing-Sicard, *Monnaies féodales et circulation monétaire en Languedoc (Xe-XIIIe siècles)*, Cahiers de l'association Marc Bloch de Toulouse, études d'histoire méridionale (Toulouse, 1961) **4**. See H Chr 334-335, 339, for the above chronology.

Meantime upon reception of the news that Raymond planned to garrison Ma'arrat-an-Nu'mān with knights and footmen from the army, the poor gossiped: "So that's it! Strife in Antioch, strife in Ma'arrat-an-Nu'mān; will there be bickering of princes and sapping of God's army in every spot which God gives to us? Let us put an end to further strife here, and for the sake of tranquility among the leaders and peace of mind for Raymond, who worries over its loss, come and let us tear down its walls."

Thereupon, even the sick and weak, arising from their beds and hobbling along on sticks, came all the way to the walls. An emaciated person could roll back and forth and push from the wall stones of such size that three or four yoke of oxen could scarcely budge. The Bishop of Albara and Raymond's friends, exhorting and pleading against such vandalism, went around about the city; but those who had scrambled from the walls and hidden at their approach were quick to resume their work as soon as the guards passed by them.[12] The more cowardly and preoccupied ones worked at night so that almost no one was too weak or sick to help in tumbling the walls.

Now the food shortage became so acute that the Christians ate with gusto many rotten Saracen bodies which they had pitched into the swamps two or three weeks before. This spectacle disgusted as many crusaders as it did strangers, and as a result of it many gave up without hope of Frankish rein-forcements and turned back. The Saracens and Turks reacted thus: "This stubborn and merciless race, unmoved by hunger, sword, or other perils for one year at Antioch, now feasts on human flesh; therefore, we ask, 'Who can resist them?' " The infidels spread stories of these and other inhuman acts of the crusaders, but we were unaware that God had made us an object of terror.[13]

At this time Raymond, upon his return from Ma'arrat-an-Nu'mān, was highly incensed with his followers; however, he

[12] Using *surgentes* to describe the rising of the sick and weak suggests Matthew 9: 6-8. The chaplain probably drew this description from the Liturgy; see *Rituale Ecclesiae Dunelmensis*, ed. J. Stevenson, *Surtees Society* (London, 1839) **10:** p. 37; see Rabanus Maurus, *On Ezechiel, MPL* **110:** c. 872. Ma'arrat-an-Numān was supposedly destroyed on January 5, 1099, or shortly thereafter, *H Chr* 336.

[13] The report of cannibalism is not an isolated one. *The Song of Antioch* has "Tafurs" sitting around roasting Saracen flesh. See L. A. M. Sumberg, "The 'Tafurs' and the First Crusade," *Medieval Studies* **21** (1959); also see *La chanson d'Antioche*, edited by Paulin Paris (Paris, 1848) **2:** pp. 5-6.

recognized God's fine hand and ordered the foundations of the
walls to be undermined when he learned that neither threats
nor force on the part of the Bishop of Albara and other leaders
could dissuade the mob from its purpose. But the food shortage
grew daily, and we ordered almsgiving and prayers for the
journey as the appointed day approached. Meanwhile, moved
by the absence of the great leaders and the weakening effect of
the famine, the Count of Toulouse ordered the Christians to
forage for food in Hispania, and he promised that he and his
knights would be in the vanguard. But some of his disgruntled
followers complained: "With less than three hundred knights
and only a small number of footmen, shall we split our forces
with some going into Hispania while others remain in the
defenseless ruins of Ma'arrat-an-Nu'mān?" And they enlarged
on Raymond's great instability.

Nevertheless, at last in behalf of the poor the Count marched
into Hispania and captured many castles, prisoners, and much
plunder. Upon his joyous and victorious return, following
the killing of many Saracens, the infidels seized and killed
six or seven of our indigent. Oddly enough, all these corpses
had crosses on their right shoulder.[14] The observers, along with
Raymond, greatly comforted by the sight, offered prayers to
the Omnipotent God who remembered His paupers. To convince the skeptics, who remained with the baggage train near
Ma'arrat-an-Nu'mān, they carried back one of the mortally
wounded who was still breathing. We saw a miracle in this
poor man, one so mutilated that his battered body scarcely had
a spot to conceal his soul. Yet he lived seven or eight days
without nourishment, all the time testifying that Jesus, to whose
judgment he would surely go, was God, the creator of the cross
which he bore on his shoulder.

14 The author's story of the mutilated bodies of the pilgrims reflects his
desire to show the significance of the Cross. There were earlier accounts of men
with the sign of the Cross on them. There is an account in Maccabees which
relates the finding of *donariis idolorum* (gifts of the idols) which implies that
the corpses had symbols on them. See II Maccabees 12: 38-41.

XI. The Resumption of the March and the Early Siege of 'Arqah

ENCOURAGED by their good fortune and the propitious omens of the crosses, the foragers left their booty at Kafartāb, four leagues journey from Ma'arrat-an-Nu'mān, and those who had friends at Ma'arrat-an-Nu'mān returned with Raymond. On the appointed day the Count, his clerks, and the Bishop of Albara departed and trudged along barefooted, calling out for God's mercy and the saints' protection as flames set by the departing Christians mounted the ruins of Ma'arrat-an-Nu'mān. In the rear marched Tancred with forty knights and many footmen. News of the resumption of the crusade caused nearby rulers to send Arab nobles to Raymond with prayers and many offerings and promises of future submission as well as free and salable goods.

We continued our march in security following their oaths and their surrender of hostages as security. But we think our guides sent to us by the ruler of Shaizar,[1] led us poorly on the first day, because we lacked everything but water at the camping site; but on the next day the same guides inadvertently led us into a valley where the cattle of the ruler and of all of the vicinity had been herded on account of fear which we had inspired. Long aware of our proposed march, the ruler of Shaizar had ordered the Saracens to flee; however, if he had commanded the entire region to block our march, it would not have been done, because we too were informed. Raymond of the Isle and a comrade on this day captured the king's courier with letters urging all the natives to flee.[2] Upon news

---

[1] Raymond probably left for Kafartāb on January 8, 1099. Shaizar was a stronghold south of Ma'arrat-an-Nu'mān. At this time it was in the possession of the dynasty, Banū-Munqidh. 'Izz al-Dîn Abu'l Asâkir Sultān was the emir of Shaizar. See René Grousset, *Histoire des croisades et du royaume franc de Jérusalem* (Paris, 1934) 1: p. 126, *H Chr* 338, 341.

[2] Raymond of the Isle is not easily identified. It is likely that he was from l'Isle Jourdain. A number of knights from this area followed the Count of Toulouse. We know that there was a Raymond-Bertrand from l'Isle-Jourdain with the Provençals. See *Histoire générale de Languedoc* 3: p. 494.

of the capture of his messenger, the king said, "My men, in place of hastily fleeing before the faces of the Franks as I ordered, come to them; and since God chose this race, I shall not stand in the way of their wishes." Then the ruler blessed God, the provider of life's necessities for those who fear Him.

The sight and capture of this unexpected large herd of cattle caused our knights and more affluent people to go to Shaizar and Camela with their money to buy Arabian horses with the excuse, "Since God took care of our nourishment, let us take care of the poor and the army"; and so we had almost one thousand of the best war horses.[3] Day by day the poor regained health, the knights became stronger, the army seemed to multiply; and the farther we marched the greater were God's benefits. Although adequately provisioned, certain men tried to persuade Raymond to turn from the route for a short time to take Gibellum, a seacoast town.[4] But Tancred and other brave and good men, blocked the move, arguing: "God visited the poor and us, therefore must we turn from the journey? Are not the past hardships of battle at Antioch, cold, starvation, and all human wretchedness sufficient? Why should we alone fight the whole world? Shall we kill all mankind? Think a bit; of one hundred thousand knights hardly less than one thousand remain, and of two hundred thousand armed footmen less than five thousand are left to fight. Shall we dillydally until all of us are liquidated? Will Christians from the West come if they hear of the fall of Antioch, Gibellum, and other Islamic towns? No, but let us march to Jerusalem, the city of our quest, and surely God will deliver it to us; and only then will cities on our route, Gibellum, Tripoli, Tyre, and Acre be evacuated by their inhabitants out of fear of the new wave of crusaders from Christendom." [5]

In the meantime along our march Turks and Arabs lurked in the rear, killing and robbing the infirm and straggling poor; and following two such incidents the Count lay in ambush

[3] Camela was the classical Emessa and the modern Homs according to Hagenmeyer and Bréhier. See *Anonymi Gesta Francorum et aliorum Hierosolimitanorum*, edited by Heinrich Hagenmeyer (Heidelberg, 1890), p. xxxiv, 10, n. 43.

[4] Gibellum was the ancient Jabala, a Syrian port near Latakia and Tortosa. We have commented on the chaplain's discourse in our book, *Raymond IV, Count of Toulouse*, pp. 113-115. We give little credence to his account.

[5] Acre was the ancient port city, Ptolemais. Tyre was a port city in Syria and was called Sūr in the Arab world. See footnote 1, ch. 13 for Tripoli.

as the crusaders marched by. On the other hand the infidels with impunity and hopeful of booty pushed behind our army as in the past; but now as they rode past the ambush, Raymond and his knights rushed upon them, threw them into disorder, confused and killed them, and happily returned to the main body with their horses. Following this experience, Raymond and a large number of armed horsemen rode in the rear guard, and as a result the enemy ceased to prey upon the poor.[6] Added to this precaution other armed knights along with the Count of Normandy, Tancred, and the Bishop of Albara rode in the vanguard so that the enemy could not rout us from the front or the rear.

It is to be noted that the Bishop of Albara left a garrison of seven knights and thirty footmen commanded by William, son of Peter of Cuniliacum, at Albara and on the advice of the Count, who wished to increase the number of knights who marched from Ma'arrat-an-Nu'mān to Jerusalem, joined the crusading army. William, a devout and faithful man in a short time with God's help caused the Bishop's interest to grow tenfold; and in place of thirty footmen he had seventy and also sixty or more knights.

We agreed in council to abandon the route to Damascus and to march to the seacoast because we could trade with Cyprus and other islands if our ships from Antioch rejoined us.[7] When we followed this course, we found that the natives abandoned their cities, fortifications, and their well-stocked farms. Then we arrived in a very fertile valley after circling great mountains only to find some peasants haughty because of their number and an impregnable castle.[8] So they showed neither peaceful intentions nor indications of abandoning their fort. On the contrary, from their hilltop they rushed down upon armed

[6] The author's description of this ambush is almost identical to that of the count's earlier ambush of the Pechenegs. See p. 21.

[7] Damascus was governed by Dukak, a Selchükid ruler at this time. See Harold S. Fink, "The Role of Damascus in the History of the Crusades," *The Muslim World* **49**, 1 (1959). William Peter of Cuniliacum was an obscure person. *HGL* **3**: p. 523, refers to a knight from Cumliac or Ciniliac.

[8] This was Krak des Chevaliers or Hisn al-Akrād. The castle still stands in modern Syria and is one of the best known crusading monuments. See René Dussaud, *Topographie historique de la Syrie antique et médiévale* (Paris, 1927), p. 92; also Paul Deschamps, *Les Châteaux des croisés en Terre Sainte: Le Crac des Chevaliers* (Paris, 1934), pp. 113-115. The skirmish and capture took place on January 28-29, 1099, *H Chr* 346.

squires and footmen who were foraging helter-skelter in fields, killed a few, and carried the spoils to their fort. Our enraged men moved to the foot of the mountain upon which the castle was built, but the natives would not come down to meet us. As a result of a council of war, our knights and footmen formed ranks, climbed the mountain on three sides, and routed the peasants. Thirty thousand Saracens occupied the fort, a fact which with its location gave them a chance to run into the fortification or on up the higher slopes. As a result they held us back for a time.

But when we yelled our battle cry, "God help us! God help us!" almost one hundred of the terror-stricken infidels fell dead either from fright or the press of their comrades at the castle gates; and, of course, outside the wall where we fought there was great plunder in cattle, horses, and sheep.[9] While the Count and his knights pressed the fight, our low-born ones became satiated with the booty; and first our poor, one by one, then our poor footmen, and finally our poor knights left the scene to return to their tents some ten miles away.

At the same time Raymond commanded his knights and people to take quarters; but the Saracens, who descended from the mountain top along with those in the castle, saw the depleted ranks of the crusaders and began to organize their broken ranks for consolidation. Raymond, neglectful of this new strategy, almost lost contact with his knights on a very steep and rocky path on which horses went single file. Confronted by this danger, he faked an advance with his men as if to attack those descending from the mountain top. In the split second of the Saracens' hesitation, the crusaders wheeled and turned to the apparent security of the valley. Foiled by this trick, the two contingents of the enemy, those on the mountain and those in the castle, upon seeing our descent joined forces and rushed the Count's men. In the press of the attack some of the crusaders dismounted while others rode headlong over steep places and thus perilously missed death, but some died heroically.

Certainly, Raymond never had been in such danger of loss of his life. As a result he was so provoked with himself and his troops that upon his return to the army he accused his knights in council with unauthorized abandonment of the battle and

[9] "God help us" is drawn from the *Breviarium, Verna,* p. 231, and Psalm 69.

imperilment of his life. Then all vowed to continue the siege until by God's grace the castle was razed. But God, the guide and protector of Christians from all disasters, so terrorized the defenders that in their precipitate haste they left their dead unburied. In the morning only spoils of war and a ghost castle awaited us.

The legates of the emir of Camela and the king of Tripoli, in camp at this time, were so impressed by the sight of our courage and strength that they begged Raymond to permit them to leave upon a promise of speedy return. Shortly after their departure along with our envoys, they returned with rich gifts and many horses. This resulted from fear which seized the whole area after our capture of the hitherto impregnable castle. In addition, inhabitants of the region sent word to Raymond along with gifts and supplications, and prayed to him to send his standards and seals until he could receive their cities and castles. I mention that it was a custom in our army to respect the standard of any Frank and to refrain from an attack thereafter. Consequently, the king of Tripoli placed the Count's standard on his castles.

As a result of this turn of fortune, the fame of the Count of Toulouse seemed to be excelled by no leader of the past. On their journey to Tripoli as envoys, our knights were impressed by the royal wealth, the rich dominion, and the populous city. Therefore, they persuaded Raymond that the king of Tripoli would in four or five days give him gold and silver to his heart's content if he laid siege to 'Arqah, a strongly defended place, one unconquerable by human force. On account of their wishes we invested 'Arqah and thereby caused courageous men to suffer unknown troubles. Sad to say, we bore heavy losses, including many illustrious knights. One of these, Pons of Balazun, lost his life from a rock hurled by a petrary, and it was because of his prayers that I have carried on this work which I have taken the trouble to write for all of the orthodox, especially those across the Alps and for you, revered head of Viviers.

I shall take care with the inspiration of God, the real author of these events, to complete the remainder of my report with the same love with which I began, and pray and beseech that all who shall hear these things shall believe in their truth. May God burden me with the horrors of Hell and blot me from the Book of Life if I, out of zeal or hatred of anyone, add anything to this book except that which I believed or saw.[10] Although ignorant of many things, I know that since my advancement to the priesthood on God's crusade, it is my duty to obey God and so relate the truth rather than fabricate lies. I wish to carry on with the same charity in my history as is exhorted by the apostle when he observed, "Charity never fails." May God aid me.[11]

During the protracted siege our ships from Antioch and Latakia, along with Venetian and Greek vessels, anchored with grain, wine, barley, pork, and other marketable goods. However, the sailors soon sailed back to the ports of Latakia and Tortosa in view of the fact that 'Arqah lay a mile from the sea, and the ships had no place to dock.[12] The Saracens had abandoned before the siege of 'Arqah Tortosa, a city well fortified by inner and outer walls and well provisioned. They left it on account of the fear which God had instilled in the Saracens and Arabs of the area, a fear which caused them to believe that we were all powerful and bent on ruthless devastation of their lands.

Yet God, unwilling to forward a siege which we undertook more for unjust interests than for Him, showered us with all kinds of misfortune. Strange enough, the Christians, who had been eager and prepared for former battles, now were indisposed or ineffectual, and the inspired soldiers of Christ who did attempt anything were either wounded or found their efforts fruitless.

At the siege of 'Arqah Anselm of Ribemont died gloriously.[13] Arising one morning, he summoned priests to him, confessed

[10] Raymond's request to be blotted from the Book of Life comes from Psalm 68: 29.; Exodus 32: 32.

[11] "Charity never fails" is taken from I Corinthians 13: 8. We shall identify the town and rulers in their sequence rather than in Raymond's style of anticipating events.

[12] Latakia was a port city, the classical, Laodicea. Tortosa, also a port city of Syria, was the ancient town of Antaradus. 'Arqah or 'Irqah controlled the routes to Tripoli, Latakia, and Homs. Apparently the chaplain did not understand the military importance of the city. The siege opened on February 14, 1099, *H Chr* 352.

[13] Anselm of Ribemont was a lord of Ribemont, a region in the valley of Oise nearby Saint-Quentin. He was the author of two well-known crusading letters. See *Epistula I Anselmi de Ribodimonte ad Manassem archiepiscopum Remorum* in *Die Kreuzzugsbriefe aus den Jahren 1088-1100*, edited by Heinrich Hagenmeyer (Innsbruck, 1901).

his omissions and sins, invoked God's mercy and told them of
the imminence of his death. While they stood shocked by the
news since they saw Anselm hale and hearty, he explained:
"Don't be astonished; listen to me. Last night I saw Lord
Engelrand of Saint Paul, who lost his life at Ma'arrat-an-
Nu'mān, and I, fully conscious inquired, 'What goes here?
You were dead, and behold now you are alive.' [14]

"Lord Engelrand, replied, 'Those who die in Christ's service
never die.'

"Again I interrogated him, this time concerning the source
of his exceptional beauty, and he answered, 'It is not astonishing since I live in a beautiful home.'

"Immediately, he showed me a home in heaven so beautiful
that I could conceive of nothing to equal it. While I stood
shocked at the sight, Lord Engelrand said, 'A much more
beautiful one is in preparation for you tomorrow,' and thereupon he ascended."

Following this widely publicized narration, Anselm on this
same day advanced to combat some Saracens who had stealthily
sneaked out of their fort, hoping to steal something or inflict
injury upon someone. In the ensuing melee Anselm fought
courageously, but was hit on the head by a rock from a catapult.
So he left this world to dwell in his heavenly home prepared
for him by God.

After this a legate of the king of Babylon, along with our
released envoys who had been captives for one year, came to
'Arqah. This king was still undecided on his choice of us
or the Turks, and so we offered his legate these terms. If he
would aid us in Jerusalem or return Jerusalem and its belong-
ings to us, we would turn over, as we seized them, all his former
cities wrested from him by the Turks. Moreover, we would
divide with him all other Turkish cities not in his domain but
captured with his aid. Rumor had it that the Turks promised
that, if the king of Babylon would ally with them against us,
they would worship Ali, kinsman of Mohammed whom he
worshiped, would accept his money, pay some tribute, and
agree to other concessions unknown to us.

[14] Lord Engelrand has not been identified. Raymond uses him to add
realism to his story. He uses tags from the service; for example, Anselm asks
Lord Engelrand, "What goes here? You were dead, and behold now you are
alive." He, no doubt, drew this from *Apocalypsis Beati Joannis Apostoli* I: 18.

The king of Babylon, because of letters from Alexius with information concerning us which we found in his tents after the battle of Ascalon, knew that our army was small and that the Emperor plotted our destruction. He had as a result of these and other things held our envoys for a year in Babylon. But now when reports came of our entry into his lands and its attendant destruction of villages and fields and all else, he informed us that two or three hundred of us at a time and unarmed could go to Jerusalem, and return after worshiping the Lord. Confident of God's mercy, we scoffed at the offer and let him know that if he did not return Jerusalem unreservedly we would move against Babylon.[15]

I remind you that the emir occupied Jerusalem at this time, because upon receipt of the news of the Turkish disaster at Antioch he laid siege to Jerusalem in the knowledge that the often defeated and routed Turks would not battle him. He received Jerusalem following the handing over of great gifts to the defenders, and then made offerings of candles and incense at the Sepulchre of the Lord on Mount Calvary.

But let us turn back to the siege of 'Arqah, for as we have reported, in the midst of our army's toil there, news came that the pope of the Turks and great hordes, who followed him since he was of Mohammed's stock, were on their way to fight us. The army was alerted for battle readiness, and the Bishop of Albara was dispatched to Godfrey and the Count of Flanders at Gibellum, a fortification overlooking the sea, midway between 'Arqah and Antioch and about two days' journey from each. Following reception of our distress call, the Duke and the Count of Flanders abandoned the siege and rushed to our aid; but in the interim we learned that it was a false rumor circulated by the Saracens to frighten us and thereby gain respite from the siege.[16] After the union of the armies, the

15 See n. 6, chap. V, for the mission to Cairo. Babylon refers to Cairo. Al-Afdal Shāhānshāh, the vizir of the Fātimid caliph at Cairo had seized Jerusalem on August 26, 1098, from the Turkish lords Sokman and Il-Ghāzī ibn-Artuk after the earlier Christian refusal to divide Syria and Palestine. Raymond reveals the antagonism of the Turks and the Fātimids.

16 Raymond refers to the caliph of Bagdad as the pope of the Turks. The 'Abbāsid caliph was al-Mustazhir (1094-1118). The real power lay in the hands of the Selchükid sultan. Albert of Aachen charged that the Count of Toulouse was paid by the ruler of Jabala to lure Godfrey and the Count of Flanders from the town. Moslem historians, on the other hand, confirm the chaplain's story that the Moslems spread the rumor. There is little reason to question the au-

Count's entourage boasted of their Arabian horses and riches, bestowed upon them by God in Saracen lands because they faced death for His sake. However, there were some who claimed that they were poverty stricken.

So because of the great number of poor and infirm, the public was urged to give a tenth of all spoils of war. The authorized division went as follows: one-fourth to the priests who administered their masses, one-fourth to the Bishop, and one-half to Peter the Hermit, the authorized custodian of the poor, the clergy, and the people. In turn, of this sum Peter gave equally to the clergy and the people. Consequently, God so multiplied the number of horses and camels, as well as other necessities for the army, that wonder and astonishment grew among the crusaders. This sudden prosperity brought such contention and haughtiness to the leaders that God's most devout Christians longed for poverty and dreadful conflict to threaten us.

The king of Tripoli offered us fifteen thousand gold pieces of Saracen money plus horses, she mules, many garments, and even more of such rewards in succeeding years. To give this offer meaning, one gold piece was equivalent to eight or nine solidi. Our money in circulation included Pictavani (Poitou), Cartensis (Chartres), Manses (Mans), Luccenses (Lucques), Valanzani (Valence), Melgorienses (Melgueil), and Pogesi (Puy), the last named being two for one of the others. In addition, the lord of Gibellum, fearful of another siege, sent our leaders tribute of five thousand gold pieces, horses, she mules, and an abundant supply of wine.[17]

Now we were well provisioned because many gifts from castles and cities other than Gibellum were sent to us. Moreover, some of the Saracens, prompted by fear or because of zeal for our way of life, anathematized Mohammed and all of his progeny and were baptized. Because of this new found wealth each of our princes dispatched messengers with letters to Saracen cities stating that he was the lord of the crusaders. Such was the ill conduct of our princes at this time, and Tancred

---

thor's version. Godfrey and Robert left Gibellum on March 12, 1099, *H Chr* 360.

[17] See Charles du Fresne du Cange, "Moneta," *Glossarium mediae et infimae Latinitatis* (Niort, 1883-1887) **4**: p. 527.

was the greatest of the agitators. You will recall that Tancred had accepted five thousand solidi and two thoroughbred Arabian horses from Raymond for his services on the journey to Jerusalem; but now he wished to join the forces of Godfrey. So he and Raymond quarreled, and finally Tancred wickedly deserted the Count.

XII. Visions and the Ordeal
of the Holy Lance

MANY VISIONS, sent to us by God, were announced now;
and I, author of this book, relate the following revelation under the name of the one who witnessed it.

"In the year of the Incarnation of our Lord, 1099, in the seventh indiction, twenty-sixth Epact, in the fifth Concurrence, on the fifth of April, at night when I, Peter Bartholomew, rested in the Count's chapel during the siege of 'Arqah, I thought of the priest to whom the Lord revealed himself with the Cross at the time of Kerbogha's siege; and as I wondered why he had never revealed himself to me on the Cross, lo and behold, I saw the Lord, the Apostles Peter and Andrew, and a large, heavy, dark complexioned, big eyed, and almost bald stranger coming into the chapel.

"The Lord then asked, 'What are you doing?'

"I replied, 'I am standing here.'

"The Lord continued, 'You were almost overwhelmed by sin like the others, but what are your thoughts now?'

"I answered, 'Lord, Father, I was reflecting upon the priest and your apparition on the Cross to him.'

"The Lord said, 'I am aware of it'; and he went on to say, 'Believe I am the Lord for whom you have gone crusading and that I underwent the Passion on the Cross at Jerusalem for your sins, and if you so believe you shall see.'

"Then I saw a Cross made of two pieces of black, round, unpolished, rough, ill-fitted wood with the exception of notched and supporting middle joints.

"The Lord commanded, 'Look upon the Cross which you are seeking,' and there upon the Cross the Lord was stretched and crucified just as in the Passion. Peter, on the right, supported Him with his head, Andrew on the left held His shoulders, and the stranger to the rear sustained Him with his hands.[1]

"The Lord continued His instructions: 'Report to my people this vision. Do you see my five wounds? Like these the cru-

[1] The description of Christ's descent from the Cross was probably drawn from art of the period.

93

saders stand in five ranks.[2] Those of the first rank fear not spears, swords, or any kind of torment, and they resemble me who went to Jerusalem, fearing not swords, lances, clubs, sticks, and last, even the Cross. They die for me as I died for them, and together we reside spiritually, one in the other. Upon their death they are seated on God's right, the place where I sat after My Resurrection and Ascension.[3] Those of the second rank are auxiliaries of the first, a rear guard as well as a shelter in case of flight. This rank, I may say, resembles the apostles, who followed and partook of food with me. Those of the third rank act as a service of supplies, furnishing such things as stones and spears to those who fight, and they remind me of those who smote their breasts and cried out against the injustice as I was hanging on the Cross and suffering My Passion.[4] Those of the fourth rank shut themselves up in their houses and tend to their own business when war arises, because they believe that victory lies not in My strength but in human wisdom. They are like My crucifiers who said, He deserves death; to the Cross with Him because He claims to be a king, the Son of God.[5] Those of the fifth rank, hearing the noise of battle, view it at a distance, seek its cause, display cowardice rather than bravery, and take no risks for me or their brothers. In fact, under the guise of caution they invite those wishing to join the fray or at least to furnish arms to sit on the sidelines; and so they are similar to the betrayers, Judas and the judge, Pontius Pilate.'

"The Lord was hanging naked on the Cross with the exception of a linen loin cloth of a neutral shade of black and red, bordered by white, red and green bands; and the cloth hung from his loins to his knees.[6] After this the Cross disappeared,

---

[2] Five ranks were common in Christian lore. It is possible that Cicero, who mentions six ranks in his "Second Oration Against Cataline," VIII-X influenced later writers.

[3] "The Lord sat on God's right," see Matthew 26:64. *Breviarium, Ordinarium Divini Officii,* p. 2.

[4] Sorrowers "smote their breasts," is similar to Luke 23:48.

[5] Christ's enemies claimed, "He deserves death." See Mark 14:64; Luke 23:21-23.

[6] The description of Christ hanging on the Cross shows Raymond's use of current ideas on his appearance. The cloth which hung from his loins to his knees was typical of the period and was much longer than the abbreviated loincloth of Renaissance art. See Alfred Maury, *Croyances et légendes du moyen-âge* (Paris, 1896), pp. 401-403; Bernard Teyssèdre, *Le Sacramentaire de Gellone,* (Toulouse, 1959); see *Planches, hors-texte* fig. 143 v, for an earlier view of Christ.

and the Lord remained in His former garb. Then I said to Him, 'Lord, God, if I report this, they will not believe me.'

"The Lord replied, 'Would you like to know the doubters?'

"I added, 'Indeed, I would.'

"Then Christ commanded: 'Have the Count call the leaders and the people together, and have them line up as if for battle or a siege, and at the proper time let the best known herald give the battle cry, God help us, three times, and have him try to complete the military array. Then, as I said to you, you shall see the ranks, and along with the other believers recognize the unbelievers.'

"Then I asked, 'What shall we do with the doubters?'

"The Lord answered: 'Show them no mercy, kill them; they are My betrayers, brothers of Judas Iscariot. Give their worldly goods to the first rank proportionate to their need; and by this act you will find the right way which you so far have circumvented. Just as other revelations came to pass as predicted, so shall these. By the way, do you know what race I especially esteem?'

"I replied, 'The Jewish race.'

"The Lord said: 'I entertain hatred against them as unbelievers and rank them the lowest of all races.[7] Therefore, be sure you are not unbelievers, or else you will be with the Jews, and I shall choose other people and carry to fulfillment for them My promises which I made to you.'

"The Lord further commanded that I relate the following to the crusaders. 'Why do you fear to bring to pass justice? Let Me ask you, what excels justice? I wish them to follow this procedure—appoint judges by families and relatives. If one commits an offense against another, let the plaintiff ask, Brother, would you like to be treated this way? If the aggressor continues, let the plaintiff charge him in accordance with his legal right. Thereupon, let the judge feel free to take all of the possessions of the defendant, giving one half to the plaintiff and one half to the authorities. If for any cause the judge equivocates, go to him and tell him if he doesn't set this right, he shall not be absolved even to the end of the world unless you free him. Do you know how burdensome an interdict can be? I commanded Adam not to touch the

[7] The Lord "entertains hatred against them." See Psalm 138: 21-22. This passage reflects Raymond's anti-Semitism.

tree of knowledge, namely good and evil.[8] He broke My command, so he and his descendants were in miserable bondage until I came as a mortal and redeemed them by My crucifixion. Of tithes, I shall say, some are to be commended because they gave as commanded, and I shall reward them and make them outstanding.'

"Following the Lord's statement, I requested Him out of the goodness of His heart that He return to me the knowledge of the services recently taken from me at Antioch. The Lord then asked me, 'Is your knowledge not sufficient for relating what you know? Yet you wish to know much more.'

"Suddenly, I grew confident of my wisdom, and I sought nothing more. Then, the Lord inquired, 'Is your present knowledge sufficient?'

"I replied, 'It is enough!'

"Then the Lord continued, 'What did I tell you? Respond.'

"Now I was blank, and when He pressed me for repetition of His words, I confessed, 'Lord, I know nothing.'

"The Lord replied, 'Go and relate what you know, and that will be adequate.' "

When we related these things to the brethren, some said they would never believe that God carried on a conversation with such a man, overlooking princes and bishops in showing himself to an illiterate yokel; and they went so far as to cast doubts on the Holy Lance. Consequently, we called together those to whom the Lance had formerly been revealed; and then we summoned Arnulf, chaplain of the Count of Normandy, and chief, as it were of the unbelievers, although a highly respected man because of his erudition.[9] We then questioned him concerning his doubts.

He replied that he was skeptical because Bishop Adhémar had questioned the authenticity of the Lance. Thereupon, a priest, Peter Desiderius, responded; "After the death of Adhémar, I saw him and the Blessed Nicholas and finally he told me: 'I now reside in the heavenly hosts of Saint Nicholas,

---

[8] The author uses Genesis 2:17 to add to his disquisition on justice.

[9] Arnulf of Chocques was the chaplain of Robert of Normandy and was called Malecorne. He became patriarch in 1099 only to be removed shortly thereafter. He was again elected as patriarch in 1112 and served until 1118 with the exception of a short interruption in 1115. This meeting probably took place on April 6-7, 1099, H Chr 363.

but because I hesitated to believe in the Lord's Lance, when, I, of all people, should have accepted it, I was led into hell.[10] The hairs on the right side of my head and one half of my beard were singed; and although I am not now chastised, I cannot see the Lord clearly until the full growth of my hair and beard returns.' " [11] Peter Desiderius told this and many other revelations which came to pass later, but we shall relate these in due course.

Ebrard, a priest, came forward and reported: "I went to Tripoli shortly before Antioch's capture, and was there keeping body and soul together when I heard of Kerbogha's siege of the crusaders.[12] Upon receipt of this news, I learned that entrance and exit to Antioch was openly impossible, and I also heard of many real misfortunes as well as imaginary ones spread by Saracen lies. So in the fear of death I took refuge in a church and fell down before the statue of the Virgin Mary. For several days, tearfully and prayerfully, I implored through her intercession God's mercy, all the time fasting and beseeching Her: 'Oh! Most kind Lady these are pilgrims, who abandoned their children, wives, and worldly goods in the name of Christ, and for You, and now they have journeyed here from far away places, and now battle for Your Son. Have compassion on them and think, Oh! Lady, of the opinion of Your Son and You, also, in their lands if You deliver them to the Turks.'

"Muttering and groaning I went over and over these and like things when a Christian Syrian came and said to me, 'Be of good cheer and stop crying'; and he continued: 'A little while ago I stood before the portals of the church of the Blessed Mary, Christ's mother, and a clerk in white vestments ap-

---

[10] Saint Nicholas was a bishop of Myra in Lycia and was supposedly tortured during the time of Diocletian. The Greeks and Latins honored him on December 6. The citizens of Bari transported his relics there in 1087 and built a basilica in his honor. Fulcher relates that the crusaders stopped at the church of Saint Nicholas in Bari to offer prayers. The cult spread to Germany, the Netherlands, and thence to America. Peter Desiderius was a priest in the Provençal army.

[11] Raymond d'Aguilers repeats in part an earlier vision of Adhémar and again shows that the singeing of his beard was the chastisement of a good man.

[12] Ebrard was an obscure priest. It is interesting to note that he supposedly went to Tripoli during the siege of Antioch. This seems improbable unless he was on a mission to arrange terms with the Tripolitans or unless movement of the Christians was very free.

peared.[13] When I asked his name and home he answered,
I am Mark, the evangelist, recently of Alexandria, and I
detoured here because of the church of the Blessed Mary.'

"I further inquired concerning his destination, and Mark
answered: 'Christ now resides in Antioch and commands His
disciples to join Him and aid in the battle which the Franks
must wage with the Turks,' and then he departed.

"When I was still doubtful, sad, and tearful, the same Syrian
reassured me: 'You must understand that it is recorded in the
Gospel of the Blessed Peter that the Christian people who are
destined to capture Jerusalem shall first be besieged in Antioch
and cannot break out until they find the Holy Lance.' "[14]

Ebrard then testified: "If anyone is skeptical, light an ordeal
fire, and in God's name and in testimony to this I shall cross
it."

Another priest, Stephen of Valence a respectable and good
person, approached and added to this testimony. "In the most
trying ordeals at Antioch, the Lord Jesus talked to me, and in
the presence of His most blessed mother, the Virgin Mary,
promised that on the following fifth day He would be compassionate and end the Christians' toil if they returned to Him
wholeheartedly. I believe the Lord was true to His word,
because the Lance was uncovered on the fifth day. Now, if
you don't believe me, I say that immediately after this vision,
I offered Adhémar as testimony to undergo the ordeal by fire
in the presence of the crowd or at his request to jump from
the highest tower, and I now offer the same to you."

The Bishop of Apt, adding to our growing list of witnesses,
came forward and testified: "Only God knows whether I saw
this in a dream or not, because certainly I do not.[15] Anyhow,
a man in white clothes stood in front of me, held in his hands
the Lord's Lance, this Lance, I say, and asked me, 'Do you
believe this is the Lance of the Lord?'

"I responded, 'Surely, Oh! Lord.' But because I sounded
unconvinced, he harshly demanded two more responses from
me and I repeated, 'I believe this is the Lance of my Lord,
Jesus Christ,' and immediately he disappeared."

[13] The chaplain has the Syrian to say,"Be of good cheer," a line which he
probably drew from Acts 27: 22-23.

[14] The instructions of the Syrian probably came from an apocryphal writing.

[15] The Bishop of Apt, a member of the Provençal clergy, had doubted the
authenticity of the Holy Lance.

Then I, author of this book, before the brotherhood and the Bishop, added to the evidence. "I was there in the church of Saint Peter when the Lance was unearthed, and I kissed its point before it was completely uncovered, and there are in the army many other witnesses along with me." I continued: "There is a priest, Bertrand of Le Puy, a member of Adhémar's household during his lifetime, who was deathly ill at Antioch. At this time Adhémar and his standard bearer, Heraclius, who had been hit in the face with an arrow and killed when he had courageously attacked the Turks in the most furious battle at Antioch, appeared to Bertrand.

"Adhémar then asked, 'What are you doing, Bertrand?'

"Heraclius answered, 'Lord, he is sick.'

"The Bishop responded, 'He is sick because he is a doubter.'

"Bertrand then whispered, 'Lord, do I not believe in the Lance of the Lord as I do in the Lord's Passion?'

"Adhémar admonished him, 'This is not enough; you should believe in more.' "

Although extraneous, because it is notable, I shall jot down the ensuing for the benefit of the worthy. "When the ill and wobbly Bertrand had to sit down before Adhémar and his lord, Heraclius, he saw as he sat there, the jagged arrow wound which ended the worldly cares of Heraclius. Bertrand then questioned, 'Lord, we thought that your wound had healed, but what is this?'

"Heraclius replied: 'That is a good question. Upon coming to the Lord, Jesus Christ, I prayed Him to leave my wound unclosed, because it brought my life to an end and so, by the Lord's will, it remains unhealed.' Adhémar and Heraclius not only reported this to Bertrand, but they added other things not pertinent to this account." [16]

Arnulf credited the Lance and confessed after hearing these and other revelations. He further promised the Bishop of

---

[16] The vision of the priest Bertrand of Le Puy reveals the chaplain's ability to write ecclesiastical literature. He first uses several witnesses to anticipate the ordeal. These men experience celestial visitations. Bertrand is deathly sick and this gives his visitor a chance to say that he is sick because he doubted the Lance. Raymond draws his description of the illness from John 11:4. Furthermore Heraclius, the standard bearer who lost his life in battle, returns with his master Adhémar and reveals that his arrow wound has not healed. This is also proper because it is in accordance with the highest wishes of a holy man to suffer. Saint Gilles suffered much the same way. See chap. 8, n. 5.

Albara to do public penance because of his skepticism; but when he came on an appointed day to a council, he stated that he fully believed in the Lance; yet he equivocated by saying that he would do penance only after consultation with his lord.

The news of Arnulf's stand caused Peter Bartholomew to become righteously indignant like a guileless but truthful man, and he blurted out: "I not only wish, but I beg that you set ablaze a fire, and I shall take the ordeal of fire with the Holy Lance in my hands; and if it is really the Lord's Lance, I shall emerge unsinged.[17] But if it is a false Lance, I shall be consumed by fire. I offer to do this because I see that no one believes in revelations or witnesses."

This satisfied the crowd, and we set the occasion for the ordeal by fire on the day of the Lord's Passion on the Cross for our salvation; and we ordered Peter Bartholomew to fast. Four days later on Good Friday as day broke, the pile of wood was started and was completed after midday. Some sixty thousand noblemen and people crowded there along with barefooted churchmen in sacerdotal garments. Dry olive branches were stacked in two piles, four feet in height, about one foot apart, and thirteen feet in length.

As the fire was started and flames shot into the air, I, Raymond, in the presence of the crowd declared: "If Omnipotent God talked to this man in person, and Saint Andrew revealed the Holy Lance to him at vigils, let him walk through the fire unharmed; but if this is a lie, let Peter Bartholomew

17 The whole story of the ordeal has created great interest. Krey notes that it is strange that the anonymous writer of the *Gesta* did not report this. Since Raymond is the only eyewitness to report the ordeal at length (the one exception is in one short passage in a recension of Tudebode), we must conclude that the very nature of his report makes his account suspect. Raymond lets us know that Peter Bartholomew was a guileless man (an expression used to describe Job—*homo simplex*). All of the details are according to the best literary traditions of ordeals—the description of the fire, the huge crowd (60,000), the religious ceremony, the supernatural visitor in the midst of the flames, the encircling bird, the emergence of the hero, all of these and more have their counterparts in other times. See H. C. Lea, *Superstition and Force* (Philadelphia, 1892), pp. 305-306. See H. C. Howorth, *Saint Gregory the Great* (London, 1912), pp. 237-238. Howorth remarks that when the fictitious is told as the truth it is often a literary device rather than the work of an uncritical mind. We do not refute the idea that there was an ordeal, but we are convinced that the description of it was a fabrication of the chaplain. Hagenmeyer dates the ordeal on April 8, 1099, *H Chr* 364.

and the Lance he carries be consumed by fire." As they knelt
the crowd responded, "Amen." The searing heat rose thirty
cubits into the air and no one could come close to it.

Then Peter Bartholomew, clad in a simple tunic, on bended
knees before the Bishop of Albara took God as a witness that
he had once seen Christ in person on the Cross, had received
from Him the above revelations as well as those from Saint
Peter and Saint Andrew, and that reports in the name of Saint
Peter, Saint Andrew, or Christ were not his fabrications. He
further added that, if he had lied, he would never make it
through the burning pile. He prayed that God would forgive
him for his transgressions against God and his neighbors, and
likewise the same to the Bishop, the priests, and the viewers
of this ordeal. Forthwith the Bishop handed him the Lance,
and Peter genuflected, made the sign of the Cross, walked into
the flaming pile bravely and undaunted, briefly lingered in its
midst, and finally by God's grace emerged from the flames.

To this day some of the observers there claim that they saw
this sign; namely, a bird, flying over Peter's head before he
emerged from the fiery grave, circled and plunged into the
fire. Both Ebrard, formerly mentioned and later a resident in
Jerusalem for God's sake, and Guillelmus Bonofilius, a respectable and excellent knight of Arles, testified to the above.
Guillelmus Malus Puer, a respected knight from Béziers,
reported that a man, dressed in priestly garments with a chasuble
drawn over his head, entered the flames before Peter did so.[18]
William stated that he began to cry when he failed to see the
man walk out of the fire, because he had mistaken him for
Peter Bartholomew and believed that Peter had been consumed
by the flames.

In the huge crowd many things were not seen, but many
revelations and acts we certainly know but shall not report
for fear of boring the reader; and besides, three capable
witnesses are sufficient for all judgments. But this we cannot
omit. After Peter crossed through the fire, the frenzied crowd
grabbed burning sticks and glowing coals so that shortly after
only the blackened ground remained. Later through these

---

[18] Guillelmus Bonofilius, a knight of Arles, and Guillelmus Malus Puer, a
knight of Béziers, are used as lay witnesses to bolster the chaplain's story.

relics in which the people had faith, the Lord performed many
worthy acts.

Peter walked through the fire, and his tunic and the Holy
Lance which was wrapped in the most exquisite cloth, were
left unsinged. As he emerged Peter waved to the crowd, raised
the Lance, and screamed out, "God help us." Whereupon
the crowd seized him, seized him, I say, and pulled him along
the ground. Almost everyone from the mob pushed and shoved,
thinking Peter was nearby and hoping to touch him or snatch
a piece of his clothing. The mob made three or four gashes
on his legs in the tussle, and cracked his backbone. We think
that Peter would have died there if Raymond Pilet, a renowned
and courageous knight, had not with the aid of numerous
comrades charged the milling mob, and at the risk of death
snatched him from them. But we cannot write more because
of our anxiety and distress.[19]

After Peter's wounds were bound up, he rested where
Raymond Pilet had carried him. We inquired what caused
him to pause in the fire. He answered: "The Lord met me in
the flames, held my hand, and said: 'Because of your doubts
of the uncovering of the Holy Lance at the time of Saint
Andrew's revelation, you shall not cross without wounds; but
you shall not see hell.' Following these words the Lord disappeared." Peter continued, "Do you wish to see my burns?"
His wounds were severe, but the burns on his legs were trivial.

Then we assembled the skeptics so that they could examine
his face, head, hair, and other parts of his body and so ascertain
the truth of Peter's revelations for which he had undergone
the ordeal of fire. Many, upon examining his face and body,
praised God with these words: "God, who freed this man from
such searing flames, flames so hot we believed not an arrow
could cross unscorched, most certainly can be our protector in
the midst of pagan swords."

Peter afterward called Raymond d'Aguilers, the Count's
chaplain, and demanded: "Why did you want me to submit
to the ordeal of fire in proof of my revelations of the Holy
Lance and God's instructions? Certainly, I know your wishy-
washy thoughts," and he revealed Raymond's thoughts.

[19] Raymond of Pilet has been identified by Bréhier as a Limousin knight in
the Provençal army. The authors of *HGL* identify him as a lord of Alais, see
HGL **3**: p. 483.

as did the Count

When Raymond denied these thoughts, Peter pinned him down: "This absolute proof you cannot deny because I found out the other night from the Virgin Mary and Adhémar the truth. I was very astonished to learn that although you entertained no doubts concerning the words of the Lord and His apostles, you wished me at my peril to hold this proof of these same revelations."

Upon Peter's detection of his lies and his guilt before God, Raymond d'Aguilers cried in anguish; and thereupon Peter consoled him: "I do not wish you to be despondent because the most Blessed Virgin Mary and the Blessed Andrew will gain pardon for you before God if you pray earnestly to them."

XIII. The Abandonment of the Siege of 'Arqah and the Renewal of the Journey to Jerusalem

IN THE MEANTIME quarrels split the army, but God, our Guide and Lord, patched up these differences so that His benefactions would not be lost. The ruler of Tripoli, a city close to our camp, upon learning of the quarrels scoffed at the demands for tribute made by our envoys: "Who are the Franks? What about their knights? How powerful are they? Think about it; the Frankish army has laid siege to 'Arqah for three months, and although only four leagues away I have neither experienced an attack nor seen a single armed man. Franks, come to Tripoli, be seen, and let us test your knights. Why should I pay tribute to unseen faces and unknown might?" [1]

This report caused public questioning: "Behold, how have we profited from disputes and hard feelings? God is reviled and we are held in contempt."

These sentiments unified the princes, who ordered the Bishop of Albara and some of the army to protect the camp while they, along with footmen and knights in customary formation, would attack the ramparts of Tripoli. On the date set when our army marched in such order, the Tripolitans, confident in their tumultuous crowds, came against us in battle array. A very solid and high wall of an aqueduct leading to Tripoli formed a narrow trail between the city and the sea, which surrounds Tripoli on three sides.

As a result the Saracens fortified the above mentioned wall of the aqueduct so that in case of reverses they could pass back and forth as if from fort to fort. Upon the sight of the Tripolitans, confident in their battle site and arms, the crusaders, footmen and knights, prayed to God, brandished their spears, and crowded together. Their advance upon the ranks of the

[1] The emir of Tripoli was Jalâl al-Mulk Abu'l Hasan ibn Ammâr. Tripoli has survived and is a beautiful city near Beirut. Raymond later formed a county there and his castle still stands. The emir was willing to treat with the Franks at first but soon appealed to Bagdad for help.

enemy was more of a procession, in that if you watched the
march you would have thought and reported that they went
forth as friends rather than foes. The Lord paralyzed the
Tripolitans with fear, and hardly anyone fled after the first
clash of arms. Now the land stank with Moorish blood, and
the aqueduct was choked with their corpses. It was a delightful sight as the swirling waters of the aqueduct tumbled the
headless bodies of nobles and rabble into Tripoli. We lost
one or two men, but the Turks are reported to have had seven
hundred killed.

After the victory our leaders returned to 'Arqah with the
booty and announced: "Today the king of Tripoli saw us,
and we in turn saw approaches to Tripoli, and we studied means
of assault. If you now agree we will let the king of Tripoli
test the mettle of our knights tomorrow." Thereupon on our
return the following day not a soul ventured outside of Tripoli.
Thereafter the king of Tripoli proposed to our commanders
that he would give them fifteen thousand gold pieces, horses,
mules, clothing, provisions, and an open public market. He
would, in addition, turn over all Christian captives if we would
abandon the siege of 'Arqah.

Emissaries from the Emperor Alexius arrived in camp at
this time protesting Bohemond's possession of Antioch in contradiction of oaths made to the Basileus. I break my narrative
by stating that Bohemond now held Antioch, for he violently
chased out Raymond's men from the towers they guarded when
he heard that the Count had set out from Ma'arrat-an-Nu'mān
into Syria. The Byzantine envoy further stated that Alexius
would give large sums of gold and silver, and that crusaders
should await him until the Feast of Saint John so that he could
journey with them to Jerusalem. It is well to mention that it
was now near Easter.[2]

2 The envoys of the Basileus arrived around April 10 according to Raymond.
See Grousset, *op. cit.*, p. 137. Runciman has a discussion of this; see Runciman,
op. cit., p. 272. Krey also deals with it. See A. C. Krey, "Urban's Crusade—
Success or Failure," *Amer. Hist. Rev.* **43** (1948): p. 243. The arguments presented by the chaplain are repetitious. One group wished to push on to
Jerusalem. Raymond, unpopular because of his Greek policy, preferred to
await the coming of Alexius. Bohemond had already shown his hand by violat-
ing his oath to the Emperor when he seized Antioch. The chaplain is openly
anxious to renew the journey and gives a compromising view of the Count
of Toulouse. The chaplain uses the dissension of the crusaders to bring charges
of sloth, pride, and envy as vehicles for his church lore. Evidence seems to sup-

Many, among whom was the Count of Saint-Gilles, argued: "Let us delay our march for the arrival of Alexius. We shall have his gifts. His presence will assure trade by land and sea, and we shall be united under his leadership. All cities will lay down their arms, and Alexius may possess or destroy them as he wishes. There is a chance also that crusaders, broken by long and constant adversities, would, if they reached Jerusalem, prefer to return to their homes as soon as they had seen its walls. Weigh carefully the number and extent of perils confronting those who are anxious to complete their vows. Let us step up the siege of 'Arqah so that in a month the garrison will capitulate or be forcibly seized. On the other hand if we decide the siege is hopeless, and news of our abandonment of it spreads afar, we, an army known for successful termination of its projects, will be mocked."

In contradiction others argued, "The Emperor has always harmed, deceived, and connived against us. Now that he realizes he is weak and we are strong through God's grace, he seeks to turn us from the Holy Sepulchre in fear that word of our success will cause others to follow in our footsteps. Let those he has often offended by words and acts beware of vain trust in him. Let us renew our march to Jerusalem, place our trust in Christ our leader, who has freed us from hopeless peril as well as shielded us from the deeds and deceits of Alexius, and then we shall, by God's promise, easily gain our dreams. Upon news of the capture of Jerusalem and open commerce, he shall respond with works as well as gifts rather than deceitful words."

The majority of the people agreed with the latter view, but their wishes and the counsel of the princes encountered difficulties. These difficulties arose because of the large entourage of Count Raymond and because he had without the other leaders braved death with the people and had made numerous large private gifts.

In this impasse we proclaimed fasting, prayers, and alms to the people with the hope that Omnipotent God, who had guided us across so many lands, would condescend to communicate His will. So the prayers of the faithful prevailed

---

port the position that the break in the upper ranks of the crusaders was not as bad as pictured by Raymond d'Aguilers.

Stephen not to be outdone

with God. Bishop Adhémar appeared to Stephen of Valence, of whom we have already written concerning his vision of the Lord on the Cross, and struck him with a rod as he was walking home one night, calling out: "Stephen."

Stephen responded, "Lord," and upon turning around recognized Adhémar.

Adhémar then demanded: "Why have you ignored so many times my commands concerning the Cross of the Lord, as well as those of our Mother, the Virgin Mary? I speak of the Cross which was in my front ranks; let it be carried in the army. Tell me, what relic is better than the Cross? Has this Cross not been stoned enough for you? Or has it not guided you to the Holy Lance? Now our Lady, the Blessed Virgin Mary, says that without this Cross you will have no wisdom."

Thereupon Stephen cried, "Oh! dearest Lord where is the Blessed Mary?"

Immediately Adhémar revealed Mary, wondrous in form and attire, standing nine or ten cubits from him along with the Blessed Agatha and a virgin holding two candles.[3] Stephen then spoke to Adhémar, who was standing beside Mary: "Lord, many are the rumors in the army, among them that your hair and beard were burned in hell and many like uncredited stories. So I earnestly request you to give me one of the candles to carry to the Count in testimony of your commands."

Then Adhémar replied, "Look at my face; do you not see it burned?" Then the Bishop walked to the Virgin Mary, learned Her will, returned to Stephen, and reported: "You cannot get your wish, but the ring on your finger is useless to you, and you should not wear it. Therefore go and present it to Raymond and tell him: 'The Virgin, very sainted Mother, sends this ring to you; and with each failure call to mind the Lady, donor of this ring, and implore Her, and God will help you.'"

Again Stephen inquired concerning instructions for his brother, and Adhémar answered: "Have him persuade the bishop-elect to perform three masses to the Lord for the souls

[3] Saint Agatha lived during the reign of Emperor Decius. She resisted the advances of the prefect of Sicily and was subsequently tortured and sent to the stake. An earthquake frightened the spectators as the pile was lighted and Saint Agatha was given a respite. She supposedly died in prison on February 5, A.D. 521. In sculpture she holds pincers and instruments of torture.

of our relatives. Our Mother Mary orders that henceforth the Holy Lance shall not be shown unless carried by a priest clad in sacred vestments and that the Cross precede it in this manner." Then Adhémar held the Cross suspended from a spear and a man clad in sacerdotal garments with the Holy Lance in his hands followed as the Bishop gave this response: "Gaude Maria Virgo, cunctas hereses sola interemisti." Hundreds of thousands of countless voices joined in the heavenly choir and the company of saints vanished.[4]

The next morning Stephen first asked whether we had the Lance, and upon seeing it broke into tears as he began to relate the above visitation, things heard and seen. Touched by this, the Count sent William Hugh of Monteil, brother of the Bishop of Le Puy, to Latakia, where Adhémar's cross and hood had been left.

In the meantime, Peter Bartholomew, debilitated by illness resulting from his crushing blows and wounds, called the Count and other leaders to him and told them: "Death comes near, and I am well aware that in the presence of God I shall be judged for all my evil deeds, words, or thoughts. In God's sight and your presence I bear witness to Him now that I fabricated nothing concerning all the things I reported to you as coming from God and the apostles. Without doubt, you will see the fulfillment of my words if you faithfully serve God." After this Peter, on the hour set by God, died peacefully and was buried on the spot where he crossed through the fire with the Holy Lance.[5]

At this time Raymond and other crusading chieftains asked natives of the region which was the best and least difficult route to Jerusalem. Consequently, some Syrians came to us, and I shall use their coming to digress a bit. Some sixty thousand Christian inhabitants have been in possession of the Lebanon mountains and its environs for many years. These Christians are addressed as Surians since they are close to Tyre, now commonly called Sur. When the Saracens and the Turks rose

---

[4] "Gaude, Maria Virgo" was used as a response and at times as an antiphon.

[5] Fulcher, who has a short account of the ordeal, takes the position that Peter Bartholomew was a fraud and that people who had formerly believed in the Lance now doubted it. See Fulcher (Hagenmeyer edition) Book I, chap. 18, p. 241. Ralph of Caen was the most critical historian of the Holy Lance story and used it in his attack on the Provençals. Peter Bartholomew died on April 20, 1099, *H Chr* 367.

to power through God's will, many of the Surians under their bondage for four hundred years or more were compelled to forsake their country and Christian law.

But if some because of God's grace defied the pagans, they were forced to hand over their beautiful children to be circumcised and trained in the Koran. Furthermore, fathers were murdered, while mothers were abused and their children snatched from their arms. The flaming evil passions of this race of men incited them to tear down churches of God and the saints, break to pieces images, gouge out the eyes of the more indestructible and use the statues as targets for their arrows. They tumbled altars and made mosques of the great churches. But if some poor tormented Christian soul wanted an image of God or a saint in his home, he had to pay for it month after month, year after year, or else see it trampled and crushed in filth. What I am about to relate is really too disagreeable. They placed youths in brothels and exchanged their sisters for wine for more lewdness.[6]

Mothers were afraid to cry in public over these and other afflictions. But why should I waste so much time on the Syrians? Surely this race plotted against the Holy of Holies and His inheritance. Had not God by His order and initiative armed brutish animals against similar evils as He did once in our presence, the Franks could have met misfortunes like those of the Surians. But this covers the subject sufficiently.[7]

The Surians, whom I have discussed above, in a meeting with Raymond of Saint-Gilles, were questioned upon the route and answered: "The Damascus route is flat, well stocked with food, but waterless for two days. The road through the Lebanon mountains is safe, bountiful in necessities, but very tough for camels and pack animals. Still another way, skirting the sea, has many passes so narrow that fifty or a hundred Saracens could hold back all of the human race. Yet it is recorded in our Gospel of the Blessed Peter that if you are the destined captors of Jerusalem, you will journey by the seacoast, although its

---

[6] The chaplain again enjoys the horrors of Turkish atrocities but in style anticipatory of later humanists he states that his task is too disagreeable. His line concerning the placing of youths in brothels is probably taken from Joel: 3:3; also see the *Breviarium Autumnalis*. Joel was read during the fourth week in November. The descendants of these Christians are modern Maronites.

[7] Raymond's reference to the arming of brutish animals refers to the later battle of Ascalon when a herd of cattle supposedly marched with the crusaders.

hazards make it appear impossible to us. This Gospel, written among us, contains not only your choice of routes, but many of your past acts and the course of future actions." [8]

In the back and forth clash of opinions, William Hugh of Monteil returned with the above mentioned Cross. The sight of the Cross so agitated the entourage of the Count concerning the journey that contrary to the advice of Raymond and other princes they burned their shelters and were the first to leave 'Arqah.

Raymond broke into tears and began to despise himself and others, but God ignored his feeling in deference to the people's will. On the other hand Godfrey, very anxious to renew the march, incited the masses. So upon leaving that hateful and abominable siege of 'Arqah, we arrived at Tripoli where Raymond, against the unanimous opposition of the leaders, tried to persuade them with entreaties and rewards to invest Tripoli. [9]

Saint Andrew now revealed himself to Peter Desiderius, a person referred to before, and commanded: "Go and inform the Count: 'Stop pestering yourself and others, because you can expect no aid until Jerusalem is first captured. Do not be disturbed over the incompleted siege of 'Arqah; and further do not burden yourself if it and other cities on the way do not fall now. Actually, a battle, in which these as well as many other cities will be conquered, is imminent. So stop worrying yourself and your followers, and in His Name give generously God's gifts to you; and further be a comrade and faithful friend to your men. God will give you Jerusalem, Alexandria, and Babylon if you do so; but if you do not, you shall neither

[8] For a discussion of the Gospel of the Blessed Peter see Clemens Klein, *Raimund von Aguilers, Quellenstudie zur Geschichte des ersten Kreuzzuges* (Berlin, 1892), pp. 72-75.

[9] William Hugh of Monteil was a brother of Adhémar. The Cross was used to offset the value of the Holy Lance. In addition, the reluctance of the Count of Toulouse to leave is not discussed by the author of the *Gesta*. On the other hand the chaplain is apparently irritated with the count and uses a series of visions to warn him. He also has the count to make every effort to block resumption of the march. Yet the author has revealed that Raymond was making plans with other leaders to resume the journey. It is quite possible that the Count of Saint-Gilles was stingy in distributing booty received from Tripoli and that his chaplain used this eccesiastical knowledge to make him the subject of moral disquisitions. See John and Laurita Hill, *Raymond IV, Count of Toulouse*, pp. 123-126, for a discussion of the chaplain's methods.

obtain God's promised rewards nor shall you henceforth have a legacy until your are in inescapable want.' "

The Count only gave lip service to these words of the priest, because he ignored them by his acts and denied them by being stingy with the great riches acquired from the king of Tripoli. Moreover, he irritated his followers with chidings and invective. Peter Desiderius related this and many other matters, part of which we report in this book.

Peter Desiderius had come to me, Raymond d'Aguilers, long before when we thought of leaving Antioch and told me that he had a vision in which a person came to him and commanded: "Go to the church of the Blessed Leontius, where you will find the relics of four saints; pick them up and carry them to Jerusalem." The person went on to show Peter the relics and the reliquary, and told him the names of the saints. Yet Peter was skeptical of the vision after waking, and prayed and beseeched God to assure him a second time that this was His revelation. So in a few days the same saint reappeared to Peter, and threatened him because of neglect of God's orders. He specified that if the relics were not moved by the fifth day of the week, great harm would come to him and his lord Isoard, Count of Die, a man faithful to God according to his light, and by his judgment and goodness useful to us.[10]

I repeated this story to the Bishop of Orange, Raymond of Saint-Gilles, and others after Peter told it to me. Soon after we came to the church of Saint Leontius bearing candles which we offered along with vows to God and to the saints of the same church. We asked God, who made these relics holy, to assign them as our comrades and aids, and these saints, rather than scorning the fellowship of pilgrims and God's exiles, out of Christian love would be bound to us and in turn would bind us to God.

On the next morning accompanied by Peter Desiderius, we came to the place of the reliquaries of saints, and just as he had related found relics of Saint Cyprian, Saint Omechios, Saint Leontius, and Saint John Chrysostom.[11] Here we also found a

---

[10] Leontius was a saint of Tripoli. There was also a Greek theologian of the sixth century named Leontius. Isoard, Count of Die, was from Die which is located southeast of Valence.

[11] Saint Cyprian (A.D. 200-258) was a bishop of Carthage who became involved in the persecutions of the Emperor Valerian. He was beheaded on September 14, 258. There was also a Christian martyr, St. Cyprian, who lived in the time of

chest with relics which the priest could not identify. Upon
questioning, the natives were at odds on identification. Some
replied they belonged to Saint Mercurius, while others gave the
names of various saints. Regardless of their obscurity, Peter
Desiderius wished to pick them up and place them with the
others.[12]

Then I, Raymond, in the presence of all the group strongly
urged: "If this saint wishes to journey with us to Jerusalem, let
him announce his name and wish, or else let him remain in this
casket. Shall we add to our burden by carrying these unknown
bones?" As a result of my words the unidentified bones were
abandoned at that time.

On the night following the priest's collection and wrapping
of the other relics in cloths and a coverlet, a handsome youth
of about fifteen stood before this priest at vigils and asked,
"Why didn't you carry my relics today with the others?"

The priest then inquired," Who are you?"

The young man continued his questioning, "Don't you know
the name of the standard bearer of this army?"

Peter admitted, "No! sir."

Upon the priest's same answer a second time, the young man
stormed, "You tell me the truth."

Then Peter replied, "Lord, it is said that Saint George
is the standard bearer of this army."

The youth then said, "Correct you are. I am Saint George,
and I command you to pick up my relics and place them with
the others." [13]

Diocletian in Asia Minor. Raymond probably refers to his relics although
there is some doubt.

Saint John Chrysostom (A.D. 345-407) in his early life became an ascetic only
to abandon this form of life and to turn to preaching. In 398 he was appointed
bishop of Constantinople. In this position he aroused bitter enmity which
eventually caused the Emperor Honorius to exile him. He died in 407 en route
to his place of exile in the desert of Pithyus.

Saint Omechios is possibly a vernacular form of Saint Epimachus.

[12] Saint Mercurius was an Armenian soldier beheaded in about A.D. 250.
There is a Saint Mercurius known in both East and West for his slaying of
Julian with a lance.

[13] The reply of Saint George, "Correct you are," is from Psalm 84:1 and was
read on the sixth day at Laudes. Saint George was a shadowy figure who was
supposedly martyred in Nicomedia about A.D. 300 and whose bones were returned to Lydda, the place of his birth. The *Golden Legend* connected Saint
George with a dragon. It seems that he was substituted for Perseus who slew a
sea monster.

However, as days passed without the priest's execution of the command, Saint George returned and harshly demanded: "Don't let morning pass without picking up my relics. Take also a vial of the blood of the Virgin Mary and the martyr Thecla which you will find close by, and then sing Mass." This time Peter Desiderius found all of these things and carried out the orders of Saint George.[14]

Before we continue our story, we must mention those men who dared to sail through the strange and vast surface of the Mediterranean and the Ocean out of love of crusading. These English, upon receipt of news of the crusades launched in the name of God's vengeance against those who desecrated the land of Christ's nativity and His apostles, set sail on the Anglican sea, and thus rounding the coast of Spain, bearing across the Ocean and ploughing through the waves of the Mediterranean, after great trials arrived at Antioch and Latakia in advance of our army. The English as well as the Genoese assured us commerce from Cyprus and other islands and so proved helpful. Daily these ships sailed to and fro over the sea thereby frightening the Saracens and thus making Greek shipping safe. However, when the English saw us leave for Jerusalem and observed the oak wood of their ships rotting with age to the point that of the thirty original vessels only nine or ten remained, some of them abandoned ship and disembarked while others burned their boats and hastened to join the march to Jerusalem.[15]

Our princes loitered before Tripoli until God instilled such a desire to continue the journey that all restraints were removed. So contrary to our custom and to the orders of the princes, we left at evening, rambled along all night, and arrived at Beirut the next day. Then after sudden capture of a pass, Bucca Torta, by our vanguard, we arrived in Acre unhindered and within a few days.[16] The king of Acre, fearful of a siege

14 Saint Thecla was a celebrated saint who received the title of "protomartyr." She was instructed by Paul and was especially popular in the Middle Ages because of her trials with fire, bulls, and other adversities.

15 The chaplain does not identify the commanders of the fleets and uses vague terms. Runciman leads us to believe that the brothers Embriaco commanded the Genoese galleys. See Runciman, *op. cit.*, pp. 275, 282. William of Tyre writes of the ships of Guinemer and his companions which came from Flanders, Normandy, and England in addition to ships from Genoa, Venice, and Greece. See William of Tyre (Babcock and Krey translation), p. 330.

16 Raymond's description of the journey from Tripoli to Jerusalem is very sketchy. The author of the *Gesta* has a much more informative account. We

and anxious for us to leave, swore to Raymond as follows: he would yield himself and Acre to the crusaders if we seized Jerusalem or if we remained in the region of Judaea for twenty days without the king of Babylon engaging us in battle, or if we defeated the above king. In the meantime the king of Acre promised friendship.[17] After this we departed from Acre one day at evening time and encamped by nearby swamps.

CONCERNING THE PIGEON WHICH BORE LETTERS FOR KILLING CRUSADERS

As is customery at such time, while some ran back and forth below the camp in search of necessities, and others sought the location of their friends' tents from acquaintances, a hawk soaring over the army dropped a mortally wounded pigeon into the bustling camp. The Bishop of Apt upon picking up the bird found a letter which it carried.

The letter ran as follows: "Greetings from the king of Acre to the duke of Caesarea. A generation of dogs, a foolish, headstrong, disorderly race has gone through my land. If you value your way of life, you and others of the faith should bring harm to them since you can easily do what you wish. Transmit this message to other cities and strongholds." In the morning when the army was ordered at ease, the contents of the letter were made public. Thus God's kindness was revealed to us, a kindness which prevented birds in flight from harming us and one which caused our enemies' secrets to be revealed.[18]

So we extolled and gave thanks to Omnipotent God and then departed fearlessly and briskly, frequently walking back and forth in the ranks. Upon news of our crossing of a nearby river, the Saracen inhabitants of Ramla abandoned their forts and arms as well as much grain in the field and harvested crops. So when we arrived on the next day, we were certain that God

---

have not translated *Bucca Torta*. The location of *Bucca Torta* is not exact. William of Tyre wrote of a "narrow pass between the overhanging mountains and the sea" which opened the way to the plain near Acre. See William of Tyre (Babcock and Krey translation), p. 332.

17 The crusaders arrived in Acre on May 24, 1099, *H Chr* 377.

18 Caesarea, the ancient classical city, was guarded by a Fātimid garrison which avoided a skirmish with the crusaders. During their four-day stay here the Christians found a carrier pigeon with a message from the ruler of Acre to the commander of Caesarea. The chaplain uses the incident for a disquisition on the kindness of God.

fought for us. Here we made pledges to Saint George, our avowed leader, and our chieftains and the public decided to select a bishop, because here we found the first church of Israel. We also felt that Saint George would be our intercessor with God and would be our faithful leader through his dwelling place.

Since Ramla is fifteen miles from Jerusalem, we had a conference there. Some argued: "Delay the journey now and turn to Egypt and Babylon; if through God's grace we could conquer the kingdom of Egypt, we would not only acquire Jerusalem, but also Alexandria, Babylon, and many kingdoms. On the other hand, if we march to Jerusalem and abandon the siege because of a water shortage, we shall never succeed."

The other group argued: "Despite a force of hardly fifteen hundred knights and a small number of armed footmen, some favor an expedition to strange and remote lands cut off from aid of our people. Consequently, we would have little chance of holding a captured city or possessing a route of escape if necessary. This is no good. Let's stick to our course, and let God take care of the siege, the thirst, the famine, and other things for his servants." [19]

[19] Ramla was also known as Rama or al-Ramlah. Here the Christians established a Latin bishopric and selected Robert of Rouen to guide it. Raymond's account of a council broken by dissension over the continuing journey to Jerusalem seems doubtful. There seems little likelihood that the crusaders could have been diverted from the siege of Jerusalem at this late stage. The Latins arrived in Ramla on June 3, 1099, *H Chr* 382.

XIV. The Siege and Capture
of Jerusalem

W E PACKED OUR CAMELS, oxen, and other beasts of burden and left for Jerusalem after taking leave of the Bishop and his garrison. In the mad scramble caused by our greed to seize castles and villas, we failed to remember and held valueless the command of Peter Bartholomew that we not approach within two leagues of Jerusalem unless barefooted. It was customary that no one seized a castle or town flying one of our standards and first touched by one of our men. So driven by ambition, many got out of bed at midnight and, unaccompanied by their comrades, captured all of the mountain forts and villas in the plains of the Jordan. But a few who held God's command dear marched along barefooted, sending up deep sighs to God because of the flaunting of His will, but they recalled not one friend or comrade from the vain course. When we approached Jerusalem on this haughty march, the townspeople struck our vanguard, wounded some horses seriously as well as many men, and killed three or four from our ranks.

In turning to the siege we note that Godfrey, the Count of Flanders, and the Count of Normandy encamped to the north and invested Jerusalem from the centrally located church of Saint Stephen to the angular tower adjacent to the Tower of David.[1] Raymond along with his army established himself on the west and laid siege to the city from the Duke's line to the foot of Mount Zion. However, a ravine between his camp and the walls prevented an even approach and caused the Count to wish to change his camp and location.

One day while Raymond was encircling Jerusalem he stopped and visited the church of Mount Zion, where he heard of God's miracles there and was so impressed that he addressed the princes and those present: "What would happen to us if we

[1] The Gate of Saint Stephen, named in honor of the protomartyr, Stephen (see Acts 6 and 7), was located to the north. The Tower of David to the west guarded Jaffa Gate. Mount Zion was situated on the southwest corner. Ravines protected the east, south, and west walls. Jerusalem was protected by Iftikhār-ad-Daulah, the Fātimid governor. He had poisoned wells, stripped the countryside of provisions, and driven out all Christians.

abandon these sacred gifts of God and the Saracens should seize them, and, perhaps, defile and break them because of their hatred of the crusaders? [2] Who knows that these gifts of God may not be tests of the intensity of our love for Him? This I do know, namely, failure to guard the church of Mount Zion zealously will cause Him to withhold like spots in Jerusalem."

Thereupon in contradiction of the wishes of the princes the Count of Toulouse ordered the moving of his camp to Mount Zion. This move caused him to suffer such ill will from his people that they neither wished to change camp nor to keep watch through the night, and so with the exception of a few who went to Mount Zion all the others remained in the original camp. But the Count daily garrisoned his stand by paying his knights and footmen large sums of money.

I shall now digress by listing some of the sacred things there: the tombs of David, Solomon, and the protomartyr, Saint Stephen. There the Blessed Mary died; Christ ate there, and following His Resurrection appeared to His disciples and to Thomas. In that very same place the apostles were aroused by the coming of the Holy Spirit.

One day, following the investment of Jerusalem a hermit on the Mount of Olives told some princes there, "The Lord will give you Jerusalem if you will storm it tomorrow until the ninth hour."

The Christians replied, "We do not have any siege machinery."

Then the hermit said, "God is so omnipotent that if He wishes, you could scale the wall with one ladder. He is with those who work for the truth."

So they stormed Jerusalem the next morning until the third hour with such siege weapons as they could improvise during the night. They broke the outer wall, forced the Saracens back to the inner wall, and a few crusaders climbed atop the inner fortification. At the very moment capture was imminent, the assault was broken off by sloth and fear. [3]

[2] The concern of Raymond of Toulouse over Mount Zion resembles the like interest of Judas Maccabeus. See *Liber I Machabaeorum* **4**: 36-61.

[3] The speech of the hermit was made on June 12, 1099, and the attack took place the next day, *H Chr* 386 and 389.

Following this reverse the Christians went foraging in the neighborhood and ignored preparations for a new attack, each preferring to gratify his palate and belly. Even more detestable was the fact that they failed to pray to God to deliver them from the many great evils threatening their very existence. New threats came from the Saracens who had covered the mouths of wells, destroyed the cisterns, and choked the flow of springs, all of which brings to mind the Lord, who "turneth rivers into a wilderness and water springs into dry grounds . . . for the wickedness of them that dwell therein." So for the above reason water was very scarce.

The Pool of Siloam, a great fountain at the foot of Mount Zion, flows every third day; but formerly, according to the natives, it flowed only on Saturday and was on other days marshy. Certainly, we offer no explanation of this phenomenon other than God's will. According to reports, when it gushed forth on the third day the frantic and violent push to drink the water caused men to throw themselves into the pool and many beasts of burden and cattle to perish there in the scramble. The strong in a deadly fashion pushed and shoved through the pool, choked with dead animals and filled with struggling humanity, to the rocky mouth of the flow, while the weaker had to be content with the dirtier water.

The weak sprawled on the ground by the fountain with gaping mouths made speechless by their parched tongues, and with outstretched hands begged for water from the more fortunate ones. In the fields stood horses, mules, cattle, sheep, and many other animals too weak to take another step. There they shriveled, died from thirst, and rotted in their tracks, and filled the air with the stench of death.[4]

This unfortunate turn forced the Christians to lug water from a spring some two or three leagues away and to water their cattle there. But the Saracens learned that our unarmed men passed back and forth through rough terrain and so ambushed, killed, and captured many of them and led away their cattle and flocks. Water brought in for sale in containers

[4] The Pool of Siloam was in the southeast corner of Jerusalem. Raymond cannot resist using Psalm 106: 33-34 to bring to mind the Lord, "who turneth rivers into a wilderness." His description of the struggle for water at the Pool of Siloam is excellent. In a saint's calendar there is a story of the intermittent flowing of Siloam and the life of Isaiah. See *Patrologia Orientalis* **21**: pp. 674-675.

was sky high, and five or six *nummi* was an inadequate sum for a day's supply of pure water for one person.

The mention of wine was seldom if ever made. The thirst, already unbearable, was made worse by the searing heat, the choking dust, and the strong winds. But why should I waste time on these mortal things? Only a few thought of God or the essentials of the siege. The crusaders did not pray for God's mercy and so we ignored God in our chastisement, and He in turn did not provide for ingrates.

At this time news of the anchoring of six of our ships at Jaffa came to us as well as demands from the sailors that we send a garrison to protect the towers of Jaffa and their ships in the port. Jaffa is almost one day's journey away and is the nearest port to Jerusalem, but little remains of the demolished place except one intact tower of a badly wrecked castle.[5] The crusaders gladly sent Count Geldemar Carpinel with twenty knights and some fifty footmen; then in his wake Raymond Pilet with fifty knights, and last William Sabran and his entourage. Four hundred crack Arab troops and two hundred Turks stood in the way when Geldemar arrived at a plain near Ramla.[6]

Geldemar drew up his knights and archers in the front ranks because of his small numbers, and confident in God's help immediately marched against the enemy. The opposition, sure that they could annihilate the Christians, rushed forward, shot arrows, and circled around. They killed four knights as well as Achard of Montmerle, a noble young man and well known knight.[7] They also wiped out all of our archers and

---

[5] Jaffa or Joffa was a port city near Jerusalem. The Christians found that the harbor had been abandoned by the Moslems.

[6] Geldemar Carpinel was closely associated with Godfrey. Shortly before his death Godfrey gave Carpinel Haifa but Tancred prevented him from holding it. See E. G. Rey, *Les Familles d'outre-mer de du Cange* (Paris, 1869), p. 264; Albert, *op. cit.*, p. 521. William of Sabran was a lord of Sabran (Gard) and accompanied the Provençals. His name appears in several charters of France. See *HGL.* **3:** pp. 490-491; **5:** pp. 687, 708, 731. There is a mistaken idea that he was a bishop of Albara. The sequence of events is well known. The report of the arrival of the ships reached the crusaders on June 17, on the next day Geldemar Carpinel and William Sabran left, and on the night of June 18-19 the fight took place, *H Chr* 392-394. We have some reservations on the time of this.

[7] Achard of Montmerle (Canton de Trévoux, Ain) mortgaged his patrimony to Cluny to furnish himself for the crusade. He marched with Hugh the Great. See Bréhier, *Gesta*, p. 14.

wounded others from Geldemar's force, but not without heavy losses to themselves.

Despite these casualties neither did the pagan attack diminish nor did the strength of our knights, truly *Christi militia,* weaken. Rather inspired by wounds and even death, they carried the attack more energetically as they underwent greater pressure. Finally beset by fatigue rather than fear, the leaders of the small band noticed a cloud of dust on the horizon at a time when they were about to break away. This sight was caused by Raymond Pilet and his men who gave spurs to their horses, and in the mad charge kicked up so much dust that the enemy believed there was a large approaching force.

So by God's grace the enemy was routed and put to flight and around two hundred were killed and great booty was captured. The spoils may be accounted for by a custom among pagans; namely, if they were in flight and hotly pursued they would fling down their arms, then their garments, and finally their saddle bags. Thus our small number of knights slew the enemy until weary and kept the spoils of those who fled.

Following the fight and the collection and division of the booty, our knights went to Jaffa where the sailors joyously received them with bread, wine, and fish. Now heedless of danger they neglected their ships and posted no seaward lookouts in the crow's nest. Soon the happy and heedless sailors found themselves surrounded from the sea by their enemies, largely due to their negligence in posting watchers. At daybreak they saw they had no chance to fight the superior force so they left their ships and bore only the spoils. Thus in a fashion our force returned to Jerusalem both victorious and vanquished. One plundering ship, absent at the time, escaped capture. Laden with booty upon its return to Jaffa, it saw the Christian fleet surrounded by a superior force. Reversing its course, it returned by oar and sail to Latakia and reported to our associates and friends the true state of affairs at Jerusalem.

We know that we got our just deserts, because we had no faith in God's messages. Consequently, the crusaders gave up hope of God's mercy and so marched down to the plain of Jordan. There they gathered palms, and were baptized in the Jordan River; and since they had viewed Jerusalem, they planned to give up the siege, go to Jaffa, and, in whatsoever manner they could, return home; but the Lord took care of the ships for His unbelievers.

We now called a meeting because of the general quarrels among the leaders and specifically because Tancred had seized Bethlehem. There he had flown his banner over the church of the Lord's Nativity as if over a temporal possession. The assembly also posed the question of the election of one of the princes as a guardian of Jerusalem in case God gave it to us. It was argued that it was common effort which would win it, but it would be common neglect that would lose it if no one protected it.[8]

But the bishops and the clergy objected by saying: "It is wrong to elect a king where the Lord suffered and was crowned. Suppose that in the elected one's heart he said, 'I sit upon the throne of David, and I possess his dominion.' Suppose he became a David, degenerate in faith and goodness, the Lord would, no doubt, overthrow him and be angry with the place and the people. Moreover, the prophet cries out, 'When the Holy of Holies shall have come, unction will cease,' because it was made clear to all people that he had come.[9] But let us select an advocate to guard Jerusalem and to divide the tributes and rents among the protectors of the city." As a result of these and other reasons, the election was not held until eight days after the fall of Jerusalem. Nothing good came from this quarrel, and only work and grief doubled each day upon the people.[10]

Finally, a compassionate and kind Lord, both for His respect and for preventing the pagans from mocking His laws by questioning, "Where is their God?" [11] told us through a message from Adhémar, Bishop of Le Puy, how to appease Him and gain His mercy. But we spread God's commands publicly without connecting them with His name in fear that the people would disobey them and so be punished more severely because of their guilt. The gracious Lord sent numerous messengers

[8] The discussions on Tancred's occupation of Bethlehem were held toward the end of June and early July, *H Chr* 396. The chaplain, sole eyewitness to report this event, gives the view of the churchmen.

[9] "When the Holy of Holies shall have come" is drawn from Daniel IX: 24-27.

[10] Albert of Aachen in his report of the meeting maintains that the Count of Toulouse and Tancred quarreled at this time. See Albert of Aachen, *op. cit.*, pp. 482-483.

[11] "A compassionate and kind Lord," is taken from Psalm 77:38.

to us but, since they were our brothers, their testimony was held worthless.[12]

At this time Adhémar instructed Peter Desiderius: "Command the princes and the public, 'Crusaders from distant lands, now here to worship God and Lord of all armies, free yourself from the filthy world, and each one of you turn your back on sin. Then take off your shoes and in your naked feet walk around Jerusalem and don't forget to fast. If you follow these orders, at the end of nine days the city will fall after a violent assault; but if not, the Lord will increase all the misfortunes of the past.' "

Following this report of Peter Desiderius to his lord, Count Isoard, to Adhémar's brother, William Hugh, and to some clerks, these confidants called a general assembly and spoke as follows:

"Men, fellows, you know the causes of the journey and our great weariness, and also that we heedlessly procrastinate in building weapons to besiege Jerusalem. Further, we not only neglect to make God friendly with us but even displease Him in every way imaginable in all things; also we even drive Him out and make Him an outcast because of our filthy deeds. Now if you think it proper, let bygones be bygones, and let a spirit of forgiveness pervade the Christian brotherhood. Following this let us lose our pride in the sight of God, walk around the Holy City barefooted, and implore the loving kindness of God through the intercession of the saints.

"Pray, we say, that Almighty God, who abdicated His heavenly lordship and became human for us and of us, His servants, and who humbly sitting upon an ass entered Jerusalem in a procession flanked by crowds waving and paying great honors only to suffer the Passion on the Cross as a sacrifice for us; pray, we say, that He may throw open the gates of Jerusalem and yield it to us to the glory and honor of His name, while He makes judgment of His enemies, who gained it unjustly, defiled the place of His Passion and burial, and who now work hard to exclude us from the great benefits of the shrine of His divine degradation and our redemption."

The above instruction met with general approval, and an order went out that on the sixth day of the week clergymen

[12] "The gracious Lord," is taken from Psalm 68:17.

with crosses and relics of saints should lead a procession with knights and the able-bodied men following, blowing trumpets, brandishing arms, and marching barefooted. We gladly followed the orders of God and the princes, and when we marched to the Mount of Olives we preached to the people on the spot of Christ's ascension after the Resurrection. At this time we exhorted them: "We followed the Lord to the spot of Ascension and since we can do no more, let us forgive those who have hurt us so that Almighty God can be merciful to us."

I need not say more on this topic. A spirit of forgiveness came over the army and along with liberal donations we implored God's mercy. We urged that He not forsake His people at the last moment after He had brought them gloriously and marvelously thus far to their quest of the Holy Sepulchre. God now was on our side because our bad luck now turned to good and all went well.

Despite many omissions of events, I cannot overlook this one: During the noisy march around Jerusalem, the Saracens and Turks walked along the top of their walls poking fun at us, and they blasphemed with blows and vulgar acts crosses placed on yoked gibbets along the walkways. We, in turn, confident of the nearness of God's compassion, because of these very abuses pressed forward by day and night the final assault preparations.[13]

Godfrey and the counts of Normandy and Flanders appointed Gaston of Béarn to supervise the laborers who were building wattles, ramparts, and siege instruments. The assignment fell to this nobleman because of ability and honesty. It proved to be a wise choice, because Gaston instituted a division of labor and speeded the job while the princes attended to the hauling of wooden materials.[14] Count Raymond also put William

[13] Hagenmeyer has dated this procession on July 8, 1099, *H Chr* 397, 398. We have some reservation on Raymond's report. The instructions which were offered were, no doubt, ecclesiastical fiction written by the chaplain. We know that many histories were to be read aloud to the people and a popular preacher could have dramatized this episode to the great delight of his audience. See Matthew 21: 1-11. Modern artists have rather absurdly drawn pictures of barefoot Christians marching around the city of Jerusalem while the Moslems watched. We cannot say that a procession did not take place, but we believe that the crusaders were not foolish enough to leave many of their forces exposed to a Fātimid attack.

[14] Gaston of Béarn was a viscount of Béarn, of Oloron, and Montaner, and lord of Saragossa. After notable service in the First Crusade he returned to

Ricau in charge of similar operations on Mount Zion and gave the Bishop of Albara the job of supervising the Saracens and other workmen hauling timbers. Raymond's men forced the Saracens from captured castles and towns to work as serfs.[15] You could see fifty or sixty of them carrying on their shoulders a building beam too heavy for four pairs of oxen to drag. But I shall not bother you with more details.

Collectively, we pressed the work, we labored, built and cooperated, and neither sloth nor unwillingness retarded our work. Only the artisans, who were paid from public collections, and the men of Raymond who got wages from his treasury worked for money. Certainly, the hand of the Lord was in our work. Soon preparations were completed and after a council the leaders ordered: "The fifth day will be the zero hour.[16] In the meantime devote yourself to prayers, vigils, and alms, and give your beasts of burden and servants to the artisans and carpenters for the work of dragging in beams, poles, stakes, and branches necessary for the construction of mantelets. Knights, the construction quota of two of you shall be one crooked mantelet or one ladder. Work hard for God, because our job is almost ended." All gladly turned their shoulders to the task, and orders went out for the attack position of princes and the disposition of siege machinery.

The besieged Saracens observed the completed siege weapons and so bolstered the weak spots that a successful attack seemed hopeless. Godfrey and the counts of Flanders and Normandy now noted the Saracen buildup, and consequently throughout the night before the set day of attack shifted their siege weapons, both wattles and towers, to a position between the church of the Blessed Stephen and the Valley of Jehoshaphat. Believe me, the disjointing, transporting over a mile, and erecting of these machines was no small job. The Saracens were thunderstruck

---

Europe and engaged the Moslems in Spain. See Jean de Jaurgain, *La Vasconie, étude historique et critique sur les origines du royaume de Navarre, du duché de Gascogne, des comtés de Comminges et d'Aragon, de Foix, de Bigorre, d'Alava et de Biscaye, de la vicomté de Béarn et des grand fiefs du duché de Gascogne* (Pau, 1902) **2**: pp. 546-549. The decision to build siege weapons had been made on June 15, 1099, *H Chr* 391.

[15] William Ricau was known as William Embriaco. He and his brother, Hugh, had commanded two Genoese galleys.

[16] Raymond's use of five days before the final assault would make this date on July 9, *H Chr* 399.

next morning at the sight of the changed position of our machines and tents, and, I hasten to add, so were we, the faithful, who saw the hand of the Lord in this.

To brief you on the move to the north, I must say that two factors motivated the change of position. The flat surface offered a better approach to the walls by our instruments of war, and the very remoteness and weakness of this northern place had caused the Saracens to leave it unfortified. The Count of Toulouse labored no less at Mount Zion to the south and received aid from William Embriacus and his Genoese sailors, who, as I related earlier, lost their ships at Jaffa, but had salvaged ropes, hammers, nails, axes, mattocks, and hatchets, all indispensable tools.[17] Now I shall leave off any more details and go on with the story of the storming of Jerusalem.

The day of the fight dawned and the assault began. But at this point we wish to add these statistics. To the best of our and other estimates there were sixty thousand combatants in Jerusalem and women and children without number. On our side we had not more than twelve thousand able-bodied men, along with many disabled and poor people; and as I think, no more than twelve to thirteen hundred knights. We introduce these figures and contrasts to show you that all affairs, be they great or small, undertaken in the Lord's name will succeed, as the following pages of my book will prove.

First, we began to push our towers against their walls and then all the hellish din of battle broke loose; from all parts stones hurled from *tormenti* and *petrariae* flew through the air, and arrows pelted like hail.[18] But God's servants, resolute in their faith regardless of the outcome of death or immediate vengeance on the pagans, endured this attack patiently. The fight was indecisive at this point, and as the machines came close to the walls defenders rained down upon the Christians stones, arrows, flaming wood and straw, and threw mallets of wood wrapped with ignited pitch, wax, sulphur, tow, and rags on the machines. I wish to explain that the mallets were

[17] The ships of the Genoese had been lost on June 18-19, *H Chr* 394.

[18] The attack started on July 14, *H Chr* 401. Hagenmeyer indicates that the towers were moved up on July 12, *H Chr* 401. His dating makes Raymond's account appear false because he mentions the rolling of the towers on the day of the assault. Runciman indicates that the towers were brought against the walls on July 14. This makes Raymond's account credible. See Runciman (*A History of the Crusades*) 1: p. 336.

fastened with nails so that they stuck in whatever part they hit and then burned. These projectiles of wood and straw thrown by the defenders kindled fires which held back those whom swords, high walls, and deep ditches had not disconcerted.

The deeds performed in the daylong battle were so marvelous that we doubt that history recorded any greater. We, assured of divine mercy, again prayed to our leader and guide, all powerful God. With the coming of night, fear settled down on both camps. With the outer wall broken and the ditch filled, speedy access was open to the inner wall, and the Saracens feared the fall of Jerusalem that night or the following day. The crusaders, in turn, were apprehensive lest the Saracens would strengthen their cause by finding a way to burn the nearby machines. Alertness, labor, and sleepless anxiety prevailed in both camps, and on our side confident hope, but on theirs gnawing dismay. The Christians besieged the city willingly for the Lord, and the pagans resisted reluctantly for Mohammed's laws.

Incredible activity in both camps went on during the night. At the break of dawn our men eagerly rolled their siege weapons into place only to be met by the Saracens, who blocked us with their machines which outnumbered ours nine or ten to one. I shall not linger on this minutiae because this was the ninth day, the day which the priest had predicted would mark the fall of Jerusalem. Despite the splintering of our siege engines by the rain of stones and the lagging spirits of our bone-tired troops, the always dominant, unconquerable mercy of God was ever present in our travail. However, I cannot pass by this interesting incident. When two women tried to cast a spell over one of our *petrariae,* one of the stones from the same machine hurtled whistling through the air and smashed the lives out of the two witches as well as the lives of the three nearby small girls, and thus broke the spell.[19]

At midday we were in a state of confusion, a phase of fatigue and hopelessness brought on by the stubborn resistance of many remaining defenders, the lofty and seemingly impregnable walls, and the overwhelming defensive skill of the Saracens. As we

[19] Raymond's introduction of the spell of the two women reveals his belief in witchcraft. The day of conquest was July 15, 1099, *H Chr* 405.

wavered and the pagans took new heart, the ever present heal-
ing compassion of God came to us and changed our melancholy
to gladness.[20] At the very moment when a council debated the
wisdom of withdrawing our machines since many were burned
or badly shattered, a knight, whose name is unknown to me,
signaled with his shield from the Mount of Olives to the
Count and others to move forward. This had a psychological
effect on our spent forces, and some revitalized crusaders
renewed the attacks against the walls while others began to
climb ladders and ropes. At the same time a youth shot arrows
ablaze with cotton pads against the ramparts of the Saracens
which defended against the wooden tower of Godfrey and the
two counts. Soon mounting flames drove the defenders from
the ramparts. Hurriedly Godfrey lowered the drawbridge
which had defended the tower, and as it swung from the middle
of the tower it bridged the wall, and the crusaders, unafraid
and undaunted, poured into the stricken city.

Tancred and Godfrey in the vanguard spilled an incredible
amount of blood, and their comrades, close at their heels, now
brought suffering to the Saracens. Now I must tell you of an
astonishing circumstance; namely, in one part of the city resistance had practically ceased, but in the area near Mount Zion
the Saracens fought fiercely with Raymond's forces as if they had
not been defeated. With the fall of Jerusalem and its towers one
could see marvelous works.[21] Some of the pagans were merci-
fully beheaded, others pierced by arrows plunged from towers,
and yet others, tortured for a long time, were burned to death
in searing flames. Piles of heads, hands, and feet lay in the
houses and streets, and indeed there was a running to and fro
of men and knights over the corpses.

Let me tell you that so far these are few and petty details,
but it is another story when we come to the Temple of Solomon,
the accustomed place for chanting rites and services. Shall we
relate what took place there? If we told you, you would not
believe us. So it is sufficient to relate that in the Temple of
Solomon and the portico crusaders rode in blood to the knees

[20] The change from "melancholy to gladness," is from Psalm 29:12.
[21] Raymond is at his best in describing bloody scenes. "The marvelous works"
with which he begins his description is drawn from Psalms 25:7; 39:6.

and bridles of their horses.[22] In my opinion this was poetic justice that the Temple of Solomon should receive the blood of pagans who blasphemed God there for many years. Jerusalem was now littered with bodies and stained with blood, and the few survivors fled to the Tower of David and surrendered it to Raymond upon a pledge of security. With the fall of the city it was rewarding to see the worship of the pilgrims at the Holy Sepulchre, the clapping of hands, the rejoicing and singing of a new song to the Lord. Their souls offered to the victorious and triumphant God prayers of praise which they could not explain in words.

A new day, new gladness, new and everlasting happiness, and the fulfillment of our toil and love brought forth new words and songs for all. This day, which I affirm will be celebrated in the centuries to come, changed our grief and struggles into gladness and rejoicing. I further state that this day ended all paganism, confirmed Christianity and restored our faith. "This is the day which the Lord has made; we shall rejoice and be glad in it," and deservedly because on this day God shone upon us and blessed us.[23]

Many saw Lord Adhémar, Bishop of Le Puy, in Jerusalem on this day, and many also asserted that he led the way over the walls urging the knights and people to follow him. It is also noteworthy that on this day the apostles were thrown out of Jerusalem and dispersed throughout all the world. On this day the children of the apostles freed the city for God and the Fathers. This day, the Ides of July, shall be commemorated to the praise and glory of the name of God, who in response to the prayers of His church returned in faith and blessing to His children Jerusalem as well as its lands which he had pledged to the Fathers. At this time we also chanted the Office of the Resurrection, since on this day He, who by His might, arose from the dead, restored us through His kindness.[24]

[22] Raymond uses *Apocalypsis B. Joannis Apostoli* XIV: 20, to describe the slaughter of the infidels around the Temple of Solomon. Modern historians repeat this Biblical reference without informing their readers of its source.

[23] This is a "new day," is drawn from Isaiah 65:17. "This is the day the Lord made," is from Psalm 117:24.

[24] The author uses his knowledge and interest in the Office of the Resurrection.

XV. Events Following the Fall of Jerusalem and the Battle of Ascalon

I SHALL PASS to other things since the above is adequate description. With the passage of six or seven days the princes on the eighth day, according to their custom, solemnly turned to the election of a king to run the government, collect the taxes of the region, protect the countryside from further devastation, and to serve as a counselor to the people. In the course of these discussions some of the clergy came together and gave their views to the princes. "We applaud your move, but since spiritual matters precede temporal ones, righteous and proper procedure demands that you first elect a spiritual leader and after that elect a secular ruler; and if you do not we shall not recognize your choice." This only angered the princes and hastened the election.[1]

I must add that the clergy was weakened at this time, first by the death of Lord Adhémar, Bishop of Le Puy, who had restrained the army, consoling them with admirable acts and sermons, just as did Moses. Then William of Orange, a respected man and bishop dedicated to our protection, soon died in Ma'arrat-an-Nu'mān. Thus with the death of these good men only the Bishop of Albara and a few others stood up to the princes. The Bishop of Marturana, who followed a crooked course when he fraudulently gained the church of Bethlehem, was captured in three or four days by the Saracens, and thereafter never made his appearance among us.[2]

Disdainful of our advice and protest, the princes encouraged Raymond of Saint-Gilles to accept the kingship; but he confessed that he shuddered at the name of king in Jerusalem; however, he said that he would not stand in the way of its acceptance by another. So they elected Godfrey and gave him

---

[1] Hagenmeyer believes that the conference was held on July 17-18, 1099, *H Chr* 408-409. See William of Tyre (Babcock and Krey), n. 1, p. 380.

[2] The Bishop of Orange had died at Ma'arrat-an-Nu'mān around September 20, 1099, *H Chr* 332. The Bishop of Marturana was a churchman from Marturana in Calabria. He was sympathetic with the Norman cause and pushed the candidacy of Arnulf Malecorne. His disappearance at the time of the battle of Ascalon puzzled the chroniclers.

the Holy Sepulchre.[3] Then Godfrey demanded the Tower of David from Raymond, and the Count countered by saying that he planned to remain in the region until Easter, and during that time he wished himself and his men to be treated properly. The Duke replied that he would abandon the Tower last of all, and so an impasse between the two developed. The counts of Flanders and Normandy favored Godfrey as well as almost all of Raymond's entourage. Raymond's men thought that the Count would return to Languedoc as soon as he lost the Tower of David. This was not the only opposition of the Provençals to Raymond, because earlier they spread malicious lies to block his election as king.[4]

Abandoned by comrades and friends, Raymond surrendered the Tower to the Bishop of Albara for judgment, only to find that the Bishop surrendered it to Godfrey without waiting for a decision. Upon being accused of breaking trust, the Bishop charged that he had done so under duress and had been manhandled. I learned that many weapons were carried into the quarters of the Bishop, namely the house of the Patriarch which was located near the church of the Holy Sepulchre. The Bishop talked about the use of physical force against him and secretly blamed Raymond's men.

Following the loss of the Tower, the Count, in a huff at his followers, flared out, saying that he had been dishonored and would leave the country.[5] So we traveled from Jerusalem to Jericho, gathered palms, and came to the Jordan. Following

[3] Albert of Aachen also states that Raymond was offered the kingship of Jerusalem. We are inclined to think that he was not, but the question remains unsolved. His later rivalry with Godfrey leads one to question the statement of the chaplain. Certainly, it would have been proper for the post to have been offered to Raymond, and as a pilgrim it would have been proper for him to refuse. Godfrey was selected as Defender of the Holy Sepulchre.

[4] We believe that the rivalry between Godfrey and Raymond over the Tower of David was not as great as the chaplain would lead us to believe. It is hardly likely that Raymond's men would at this time have deserted him in behalf of Godfrey. The Tower of David was left in the hands of the Bishop of Albara who turned it over to Godfrey. Shortly thereafter, on July 28, 1099, Raymond left for his trip to the Jordan River, *H Chr* 411. After his trip to the Jordan, Raymond returned to aid Godfrey at Ascalon. So it is possible that the chaplain uses Raymond for an illustration of a dishonored man shaking the dust from his feet and leaving Jerusalem. Godfrey's contention that he was a liege lord may also have conflicted with Raymond's idea that Jerusalem was a possession of the church.

[5] The author's description of Raymond's anger is taken from Psalm 2:13. He often makes Raymond the subject of his church knowledge.

the instructions of Peter Bartholomew, we made a raft of small branches, placed Raymond on it, and paddled across the river. We then ordered the assembled crowd to pray for the lives of the Count and the other princes. With Count Raymond clad only in shirt and new pants, we carried out the order concerning baptism, but why God's man, Peter Bartholomew, issued such an order we have not the slightest idea until the present time.[6]

Upon our return to Jerusalem after this task, Arnulf, chaplain of the Count of Normandy, was elected by some as patriarch contrary to the wishes of the good clergymen, who objected on the grounds that he was not a subdeacon and was of priestly origin.[7] To cap it all he was accused of being a philanderer on the journey, even to the point that he was the object of smutty stories. Needless to say, the ambitious Arnulf ignored canonical decrees, his disgraceful birth and lack of conscience, berated the good clergy, and had himself elevated to the patriarchal seat to the accompaniment of hymns, chants, and great applause of the people. Arnulf was not frightened by the divine punishment of the Bishop of Marturana, the inciter and director of Arnulf's elevation, for he continued to take benefices from clergymen who had altars in the Lord's Sepulchre or from those who received fees for its care.

Once in power Arnulf sought to locate with the help of the inhabitants, the Cross worshiped by pilgrims before the Turkish capture of Jerusalem. They knew nothing of its location, going so far as to prove their words by oath and other signs, but they were finally forced to say, "Revelation shows that you are God's chosen people, that you have been freed from trials and given Jerusalem and many other cities not by your great strength but by a wrathful God who blinded the blasphemers. The Lord, your leader, threw open the gates of impregnable cities and won terrifying battles for you. Since God is on your side why should we obstinately hide His relics from you." Then after leading the crusaders to a hall in the church, they uncovered and surrendered the Cross.[8] So we were glad and praised and thanked almighty God who not only restored to us

---

[6] The fact that the author questioned the wisdom of Peter's baptismal instructions leads us to believe that he was questioning his source of information.

[7] Arnulf's election as patriarch took place on August 1, 1099, *H Chr* 413.

[8] The Holy Cross was found on August 5, 1099, *H Chr* 415.

the city of His Passion but the symbols of His crucifixion and victory so that we might clasp Him more closely in the arms of faith, surer because we now saw the relics of our salvation.

At this time, as we have previously reported, Godfrey held Jerusalem by agreement, and Raymond was exasperated by grief and injustice over the loss of the Tower of David, undoubtedly the key to the Kingdom of Judaea. As a result he made plans to return with a great part of his Provençals. However, news came that the king of Babylon had arrived in Ascalon with a large force of pagans with the purpose of storming Jerusalem, killing all of the Franks twenty years of age and above, and capturing the rest along with their women. He would, so rumor held, mate the young Frankish males with women of his race and the Frankish women with young males of his land and thereby breed a warrior race from Frankish stock.[9]

His grandiose schemes led him to boast he would give the same treatment to Antioch and Bohemond; further, that he would wear the crown of Damascus and the remaining cities. Moreover, upon due consideration of his mighty hosts of soldiers and knights, he held the Turks were nothing and the Franks, conquerors of the Turks, were nothing. Still unsatisfied, he blasphemed God by saying that he would destroy the Lord's birthplace, the manger where the Lord had lain, the place of the Passion and Golgotha, purportedly the spot where blood gushed from the crucified Lord, the Lord's burial grave, and all other sacred spots in Jerusalem and its environs.[10] He further boasted that he would unearth these relics, break them into small pieces, and scatter their dust over the sea so that the Franks would no longer search beyond their lands for relics of the Lord now lost in the oblivion of the sea.[11]

Our princes and clergy assembled upon news of this and other rumors concerning the vast hordes of this tyrant gathered at Ascalon, a city removed from us by a journey of a day and one half. The assembled crusaders marched barefooted before the

[9] Ascalon was the classical Ashkelon located some forty miles from Jerusalem. Theoretically it was held by the Fātimid caliph of Cairo, al-Musta'li (1094-1100). The actual power lay in the hands of the vizir, al-Afdal Shāhānshāh. The chaplain writes of the king of Babylon. News of the approach must have come between August 6 and August 9.

[10] "The manger where the Lord had lain," is taken from Luke 2:7.

[11] "Scatter their dust" is from Psalm 17: 43.

Holy Sepulchre and tearfully begged mercy from the Lord, asking Him to free His people whom He had made conquerors in the past. They also beseeched Him not to permit the further profanation of the place of His sanctification, which had just been purified for His name's sake. Then we came to the Temple of the Lord barefooted, imploring His mercy with songs, hymns, and saintly treasures, and there in soul and body poured forth our prayers before God. We urged that He remember the pouring forth of His blessing in the same place: "If your people have sinned against you and changing have done penance and coming have prayed in this place, listen to them from heaven, Oh! Lord, and free them from the hands of their enemies." [12]

Following the blessing of the Bishop, the leaders drew up the battle plans and means of protection of Jerusalem. Then Godfrey and his knights departed to verify the rumors regarding the emir, and upon arriving at the plains of Ramla dispatched the Bishop of Marturana to report to the counts in Jerusalem on the state of affairs. Now certain of a battle, the leaders issued a call to the able bodied, prayed to God, marched out of Jerusalem in full armor carrying the Holy Lance, and on the same day came to the plains. On the following day our united armies moved forward in squadrons with guards drawn up on all sides.[13]

At sundown we approached a river which is on the road from Jerusalem to Ascalon, and we saw Arabs pasturing flocks of sheep and large herds of cattle and camels. So we sent two hundred knights to reconnoiter, because the large number of Arabs and livestock made us believe that a fight would ensue. In the meantime, as we have written, we marched in nine ranks, three to the rear, three to the front, and three in the middle so that attack would be met in three ranks with the middle one always available to bolster the others. The Arab

[12] This scene along with the discourse was probably inspired by I Kings 8.
[13] Godfrey left to scout on August 9, the crusaders approached Ascalon on August 11, 1099, and on the following day the battle took place, H Chr 418, 420, 421. The Holy Lance was later carried by the Count of Toulouse on the Crusade of 1101 and used by the Bishop of Milan to inspire the crusaders. The fate of the Lance was long debated. Matthew of Edessa claimed that the lance used by the Bishop of Milan was not the authentic one. Albert of Aachen stated that it was lost in the Crusade of 1101. See Steven Runciman, "The Holy Lance Found at Antioch," Analecta Bollandiana 68 (1950).

herdsmen fled at the sight of our knights, but had God favored them as He did us they, no doubt, would have defended their animals. Actually they numbered three thousand while our army possibly had twelve hundred knights and no more than nine thousand footmen. Following their flight we seized unbelievable amounts of booty, and killed and captured a few Arabs. Since it was late in the day we pitched camp, and then we compelled the captives to reveal their plans, state of preparations, and their numbers. The captives stated that the Arabs wished to invest Jerusalem and drive out, take captive, or kill the Franks. They added that the emir, who camped five leagues away, would march against us the next day. The herders ventured no absolute estimate of the size of their army since it increased daily. Regarding their role, they said that they were herders who planned to sell their animals to the Babylonian army.

The crusaders, ready for the ensuing conflict, forgave one another sins of commission and omission, and became so stirred that they hardly credited reports of the preparedness of the enemy. In their assurance they believed the Arabs to be more timid than deer and more innocuous than sheep. This assurance was born from our belief that God was with us as in other trials and that on account of the pagan's blasphemy He would on His own initiative punish them even if our cause was weak. Thus we preferred to think of God as defender and ourselves as His helpers.

Orders then were given throughout the army that all be prepared for battle at dawn, that each one join the forces of his leader, and that no one should touch booty until after the battle, under pain of excommunication. We spent a wretched night with no tents, little bread, no wine, very little grain and salt; but at least the meat supply was plentiful as sand, and so we ate meat and used mutton for bread.

At the crack of dawn the alert army was called to battle ranks by the blare of trumpets and horns. Thus we set out at daybreak with guards arranged on all sides as previously reported and moved toward the camp of Mohammed. The Arabs remained in their camp in the belief that at news of their coming we would remain close to our walls. Reports had come to them of the slaughter and flight of the herders and brought this response: "The Franks came for booty and will now return."

Actually they had daily reports on the desertions in Jerusalem, the small size of our army, and the enfeebled state of our people and horses. Confident in their size and strength, they were sure that they could drown us and our camp in their spit. Their stargazers and soothsayers, so we heard, advised against moving camp or fighting until the seventh day of the week, with the warning that an earlier date would be disadvantageous.

We moved forward in nine ranks, as stated above, and God multiplied his army to the point that we seemed to equal the Arab forces. This miracle came when the animals we had freed formed herds, and without a directing hand followed us, stood when we stood, ran when we ran, and marched forward when we marched forward. We could neither estimate the amount of costly goods nor compute the sum total of arms and tents seized. The Arabs upon seeing the slaughter of many of their comrades, the eager and secure ransacking of their camp, gave up the fight and decided, "Since we must flee, why delay? If today, these Christians, exhausted from the march and almost dead tired from hunger and thirst, smashed our forces with one attack, what could they do refreshed, restored and victorious against us half alive, weakened, and terrified?"

Consequently, with morale broken the Arabs with a few exceptions returned to Ascalon, which lay about a mile from our camp. Raymond decided to send Bohemond, a Turk, to the emir with a plan for peace but reminded him that he had been reluctant to free Jerusalem and had fought us.[14] Bohemond, at the same time, was to size up the situation, and to see whether the emir planned to flee or to fight, and how he reacted to his defeat. Bohemond, although a Turk, was multilingual, clever and shrewd as well as loyal to us. He was called Bohemond because the great Bohemond received him at the baptismal font when he turned apostate and came to us with his wife and arms.

The Book of Raymond d'Aguilers happily ends.

[14] The scribe probably started on another story at this point.

IMPORTANT DATES

Ca. 1041-1042. Birth of Raymond of Saint-Gilles.

August 15, 1095. Meeting of Pope Urban II and Adhémar of Le Puy at Notre Dame du Puy.

November 27, 1095. Urban preaches the First Crusade in Clermont.

November 28, 1095. Ambassadors of Raymond of Saint-Gilles indicate the acceptance of the Cross by their master.

July 12, 1096. Raymond of Saint-Gilles makes a cession in favor of the abbey of Saint-Gilles in the presence of Urban.

October, 1096. Departure of the Provençals.

January, 1097. Treaty of the Provençals and Bodin at Scutari.

February (middle), 1097. Pechenegs' seizure of Adhémar.

April 12, 1097. Provençal attack on Roussa.

April 18, 1097. Ambassadors of Alexius arrive at Rodosto.

April 20, 1097. Skirmish between the Provençals and the Greeks.

April 22-26, 1097. Conversations of Raymond of Saint-Gilles and Alexius.

May 10, 1097. Raymond leaves Constantinople.

May 14, 1097. Beginning of the siege of Nicaea.

May 16, 1097. Arrival of the Provençals at the siege of Nicaea.

June 10, 1097. Sapping of the tower of Gonates.

June 19, 1097. Surrender of Nicaea.

June 28, 1097. Provençals depart Nicaea.

July 1-October 20, 1097. Battle of Dorylaeum and journey to Antioch.

August 5, 1097. Illness of Raymond of Saint-Gilles.

October 20-22, 1097. Opening of the siege of Antioch.

November 17, 1097. Arrival of the Genoese vessels at Saint-Simeon.

December 29, 1097. Men of Yaghī Sīyan attack the crusaders.

January 2, 1098. Time set by Adhémar for fasting and alms giving.

February 9, 1098. Defeat of reinforcements of Ridvan. Arrival of emissaries of al-Afdal.

March 4, 1098. Arrival of Edgar Atheling.

March 20, 1098. Completion of La Mahomerie.

April 5, 1098. Council of crusaders held to fortify a castle on the site of the old monastery of Saint-George.

May 25, 1098. Bohemond suggests that the prince who seized Antioch should gain possession of it.

May 29, 1098. Council of princes makes an agreement with Bohemond.

June 2, 1098. Bohemond reveals his plan to seize Antioch with the help of Firūz.

June 3, 1098. Antioch falls.

June 28, 1098. Defeat of Kerbogha.

July 3, 1098. Council of crusaders postpones march to Jerusalem.

August 1, 1098. Death of Adhémar.

September 14, 1098. Raymond assists Godfrey at 'Azāz.

October, 1098. Provençal capture of Albara.

November 5, 1098. Council of the crusaders in the church of Saint Peter at Antioch.

December 11-12, 1098. Capture of Ma'arrat-an-Nu'mān.

December 29, 1098. Meeting of Bohemond and Raymond.

January 4, 1099. Meeting of the princes to debate resumption of the march to Jerusalem.

January 13, 1099. Raymond leaves Ma'arrat-an-Nu'mān.

January 25, 1099. Crusaders are attacked from ambush.
February 4, 1099. Reception of emissaries of the atabeg of Homs and the emir of Tripoli.
February 14-May 13, 1099. Siege of 'Arqah.
April 8, 1099. Ordeal of the Holy Lance.
April 10-11, 1099. Ambassadors of Alexius make complaints over Bohemond's seizure of Antioch.
May 16, 1099. Crusaders leave Tripoli.
June 3, 1099. Christians enter Ramla.
June 7, 1099. Crusaders approach Jerusalem.
June 9, 1099. Raymond Pilet and Raymond of Turenne make a successful raid.
June 17, 1099. Arrival of Genoese ships at Jaffa.
July 8, 1099. Procession of Christians around Jerusalem.
July 13-15, 1099. Final assault and capture of Jerusalem.
July 22, 1099. Election of Godfrey.
July 28, 1099. Raymond of Saint-Gilles leaves Jerusalem.
August 12, 1099. Battle of Ascalon.

BIBLIOGRAPHY

Manuscripts

MS. Latin 14,378, Bibliothèque Nationale, Paris.
MS. Latin 5131, Bibliothèque Nationale, Paris.
MS. Latin 5511 A, Bibliothèque Nationale, Paris.
MS. Latin 1102, Bibliothèque de l'Arsenal, Paris.
MS. Latin Add. 8927, British Museum, London.
MS. Latin 262, Bibliothèque de la ville, Clermont-Ferrand.
MS. Latin 261, Burgerbibliothek, Berne.

Sources

Acta Sancti Brendani, edited by Patrick F. Moran (Dublin, 1872).
Acta sanctorum quotque toto orbe coluntur, vel a Catholicis scriptoribus cele-brantur (Antwerp, Paris, Rome, Brussels, 1643-1940).
The Alexiad of the Princess Anna Comnena, translated by Elizabeth A. S. Dawes (London, 1928).
Albertus Aquensis, *Historia Hierosolymitana* in *Recueil des historiens des croi-sades: historiens occidentaux* 4 (Paris, 1879). Hereafter cited *RHC Occ.*
Anonymi gesta Francorum et aliorum Hierosolimitanorum, edited by Heinrich Hagenmeyer (Heidelberg, 1890).
Breviarium Romanum (4 v. Ratisbonae, 1923).
COMNENA, ANNA. 1937-1945. *Alexiade. Règne de l'empereur Alexis I Comnène (1081-1118)*, edited by B. Leib in *Collection byzantine de l'Association Guillaume Budé* (Paris).
La Chanson d'Antioche, edited by Paulin Paris (2 v. Paris, 1848).
Fulcherius Carnotensis, *Historia Hierosolymitana. Gesta Francorum Iherusalem Peregrinantium* in *RHC Occ* 3 (Paris, 1866).
—— *Historia Hierosolymitana. Gesta Francorum Iherusalem Peregrinantium*, edited by Heinrich Hagenmeyer (Heidelberg, 1913).
The Golden Legend of Jacobus de Voragine, translated by G. Ryan and H. Rip-perger, 1 (New York, 1941).
HAGENMEYER, HEINRICH. 1901. *Die Kreuzzugsbriefe aus den Jahren 1088-1100* (Innsbruck).
Histoire anonyme de la première croisade, edited and translated by Louis Bréhier (Paris, 1924).
KREY, A. C. 1958. *The First Crusade* (Gloucester).
Patrologiae cursus completus: Series Latina, edited by J. P. Migne (Paris, 1844-1864). Hereafter cited as *MPL*.
Patrologiae Orientalis, edited by R. Graffin and F. Nau (Paris, 1907-).
Notitiae duae Lemovicensis de praedicatione crucis in Aquitania in *RHC Occ* 5 (Paris, 1895).
Radulphus Cadomensis, *Gesta Tancredi in expeditione Hierosolymitana* in *RHC Occ* 3 (Paris, 1866).
Raimundus de Aguilers, *Historia Francorum qui ceperunt Iherusalem* in *RHC Occ* 3 (Paris, 1866).
Rituale Ecclesiae Dunelmensis, edited by J. Stevenson, in *Surtees Society* 10 (London, 1839).

THORPE, BENJAMIN, editor and translator. 1844-1846. *The Homilies of the Anglo-Saxon Church* (2 v. London).

Tudebodus, Petrus, *Historia de Hierosolymitano itinere* in *RHC Occ* 3 (Paris, 1866).

Willelmus Tyrensis archiepiscopus, *Historia rerum in partibus transmarinis gestarum* in *RHC Occ* 1 (Paris, 1844).

William of Tyre, *A History of Deeds Done Beyond the Seas,* translated by E. A. Babcock and A. C. Krey (New York, 1943).

Works

ALPHANDÉRY, P., and A. DUPRONT. 1954. *La chrétienté et l'idée de croisade* (Paris).

ANDRESSOHN, J. C. 1947. *The Ancestry and Life of Godfrey of Bouillon* (Bloomington).

ARBELLOT, ABBÉ. 1881. *Les Chevaliers Limousins à la première croisade* (Paris).

ATIYA, A. S. 1962. *The Crusade: Historiography and Bibliography* (Bloomington).

BALDWIN, MARSHALL W. 1940. "Some Recent Interpretations of Pope Urban's Eastern Policy." *Catholic Hist. Rev.* 25.

BISHOP, EDMUND. 1918. *Liturgica Historica* (Oxford).

BRUNDAGE, JAMES A. 1959. "Adhémar of Puy. The Bishop and His Critics," *Speculum* 34.

—— 1960. "An Errant Crusader: Stephen of Blois," *Traditio* 16

—— 1964. "Recent Crusade Historiography: Some Observations and Suggestions." *Catholic Hist. Rev.* 49.

CASTAING-SICARD, MIRELLE. 1961. *Monnaies féodales et circulation monétaire en Languedoc* (Xe-XIIIe siècles) in *Cahiers de l'association Marc Bloch de Toulouse, études d'histoire méridionale* (Toulouse).

DALY, WILLIAM. 1960. "Christian Fraternity, the Crusaders, and the Security of Constantinople, 1097-1204: The Precarious Survival of an Ideal." *Mediaeval Studies* 22.

DAVID, CHARLES W. 1920. *Robert Curthose, Duke of Normandy* (Cambridge).

DESCHAMPS, PAUL. 1934. *Les Châteaux des croisés en Terre Sainte: le Crac des Chevaliers* (Paris).

DEVIC, DOM. CL., and DOM. J. VAISSETE. 1872-1893. *Histoire générale de Languedoc* (15 v., Toulouse).

DUNCALF, FREDERIC. 1928. "The Pope's Plan for the First Crusade." *The Crusades and Other Historical Essays Presented to Dana C. Munro* (New York).

DUSSAUD, RENÉ. 1927. *Topographie historique de la Syrie antique et médiévale* (Paris).

ERDMANN, C. 1935. *Die Entstehung des Kreuzzugsgedankens* (Stuttgart).

FINK, HAROLD S. 1959. "The Role of Damascus in the History of the Crusades." *The Muslim World* 49.

GAUSSIN, PIERRE-ROGER. 1960. *L'Abbaye de la Chaise-Dieu (1043-1518)* (Paris).

GOLB, NORMAN. 1966. "New Light on the Persecution of French Jews at the Time of the First Crusade." *Proc. Amer. Acad. Jewish Research* 34.

GROUSSET, RENÉ. 1934-1936. *Histoire des croisades et du royaume franc de Jerusalem* (3 v., Paris).

HAGENMEYER, HEINRICH. 1902-1911. "Chronologie de la première croisade, 1094-1100." *Revue de l'Orient latin* 6-8.

—— 1879. *Peter der Eremite. Ein kritischer Beitrag zur Geschichte des ersten Kreuzzuges* (Leipzig).

HERMANNSON, HALLDÓR. 1936. "The Problem of Wineland." *Islandica* 25.

HILL, JOHN HUGH. 1951. "Raymond of Saint-Gilles in Urban's Plan of Greek and Latin Friendship." *Speculum* **26**.

HILL, JOHN HUGH and LAURITA L. 1953. "The Convention of Alexius Comnenus and Raymond of Saint-Gilles." *Amer. Hist. Rev.* **58**.

HILL, JOHN HUGH and LAURITA L. 1954. "Justification historique du titre de Raymond de Saint-Gilles: 'Christiane milicie excellentissimus princeps.' " *Annales du Midi* **66**.

HILL, JOHN HUGH and LAURITA L. 1955. "Contemporary Accounts and the Later Reputation of Adhémar, Bishop of Puy." *Medievalia et Humanistica* **9**.

HILL, JOHN HUGH and LAURITA L. 1959. *Raymond IV de Saint-Gilles 1041 (ou 1042)-1105. Bibliothèque Méridionale, Série historique* **35** (Toulouse).

HILL, JOHN HUGH and LAURITA L. 1960. "L'Allégorie chrétienne dans les récits relatifs au Wineland." *Le Moyen Age* n. 1-2.

HILL, JOHN HUGH and LAURITA L. 1962. *Raymond IV, Count of Toulouse* (Syracuse).

HOWORTH, SIR HENRY H. 1912. *Saint Gregory the Great* (London).

JAURGAIN, JEAN DE. 1902. *La Vasconie, étude historique et critique sur les origines du royaume de Navarre, du duché de Gascogne, des comtés de Comminges d'Aragon, de Foix, de Bigorre, d'Alava et de Biscaye, de la vicomté de Béarn et des grand fiefs du duché de Gascogne* **2** (Pau).

KLEIN, CLEMENS. 1892. *Raimond von Aguilers, Quellenstudie zur Geschichte des ersten Kreuzzuges* (Berlin).

KNAPPEN, MARSHALL M. 1928. "Robert II of Flanders in the First Crusade." *The Crusades and other Historical Essays Presented to Dana C. Munro* (New York).

KREY, A. C. 1958. *The First Crusade* (Gloucester).

—— 1948. "Urban's Crusade—Success or Failure." *Amer. Hist. Rev.* **53**.

LA MONTE, JOHN L. 1940. "Some Problems in Crusading Historiography." *Speculum* **15**.

LEA, H. C. 1892. *Superstition and Force* (Philadelphia).

MAURY, ALFRED. 1896. *Croyances et légendes du Moyen Âge* (Paris).

MAYER, HANS EBERHARD. 1960. *Bibliographie zur Geschichte der Kreuzzüge* (Hannover).

—— 1960. "Zur Beurteilung Adhemars von Le Puy." *Deutsches Archiv* n. 2.

MUNRO, DANA C. 1906. "The Speech of Pope Urban II at Clermont, 1095." *Amer. Hist. Rev.* **11**.

NICHOLSON, ROBERT LAWRENCE. 1940. *Tancred: A Study of His Career and Work in Their Relation to the First Crusade and the Establishment of the Latin States in Syria and Palestine* (Chicago).

PAPON, JEAN-PIERRE. 1778. *Histoire générale de Provence* **2** (Paris).

PORGES, WALTER. 1946. "The Clergy, the Poor, and the Non-Combatants on the First Crusade." *Speculum* **21**.

RÉAU, LOUIS. 1955. *Iconographie de l'art Chrétien* (Paris).

REY, EDOUARD G. 1869. *Les Familles d'outre-mer, de du Cange* (Paris).

RIANT, PAUL. 1881. "Inventaire critique des lettres historiques des croisades." *Archives de l'Orient Latin* **1**.

ROUSSET, P. 1945. *Les Origines et les caractères de la première croisade* (Neuchâtel).

RUNCIMAN, STEVEN, 1951. *A History of the Crusades* **1** (Cambridge).

—— 1950. "The Holy Lance Found at Antioch." *Analecta Bollandiana* **68**.

SETTON, KENNETH M. 1955. *A History of the First Crusade, The First Hundred Years* **1** (ed. Marshall Baldwin, Philadelphia).

SMAIL, R. C. 1956. *Crusading Warfare (1097-1193). A Contribution to Medieval Military History* (Cambridge).

SUMBERG, L. A. M. 1959. "The 'Tafurs' and the First Crusade." *Medieval Studies* **21**.

TEYSSÈDRE, BERNARD. 1959. *Le Sacramentaire de Gellone* (Toulouse).

VILLEY, M. 1942. *La Croisade. Essai sur la formation d'une théorie juridique* (Paris).

WILLARD, RUDOLPH. 1935. *Two Apocrypha in Old English Homilies* in *Beiträge zur Englischen Philologie* **30**.

YEWDALE, RALPH BAILEY. 1917. *Bohemond I, Prince of Antioch* (Princeton).

Index

Áchard of Montmerle, loses life, 119

Acre, arrival of the crusaders, 113

Adhémar, bishop of Le Puy, 15; attacked and injured by a band of Pechenegs, 21; arrives at Constantinople, 24; troops sap a tower at Nicaea, 26; loses standard, 34; interviews Peter Bartholomew, 51; orders gates of Antioch closed, 56, 57; participates in battle against Kerbogha, 61; dies at Antioch, 66; appears in a vision, 66; appears in a vision to Peter Desiderius, 96, 97; appears to Bertrand, 99; reported in the vanguard of attackers of Jerusalem, 128

al-Afdal Shāhānshāh, vizir of Egypt, sends embassy to Antioch, 40, 41; sends a legate to 'Arqah to offer terms to the Christians, 89; threatens the Christians, 132; defeated at Ascalon, 135

Albara, captured, 73; Peter of Narbonne made bishop, 73

Aleppo, base of Rîdvan's attacks on Antioch, 32

Alexius Comnenus, Byzantine emperor, promises security to the Provençals, 18; demands oath and homage from Raymond of Saint-Gilles, 23; angers the Latins after the fall of Nicaea, 26, 27; rumor of his approach to Antioch, 37; emissaries protest Bohemond's seizure of Antioch and urge crusaders to await the coming of Alexius, 105

Anselm of Ribemont, loses life at 'Arqah, 88, 89

Antioch, crusaders besiege, 30; description, 30, 31; falls, 47, 48

Apt, bishop, reports visions, 70, 98; finds a letter from the ruler of Acre, 114

Arnulf of Chocques, chaplain of the Count of Normandy, questions the authenticity of the Holy Lance, 96; credits the Lance but refuses to do penance, 99, 100; elected patriarch of Jerusalem, 131

'Arqah, Latins besiege, 87

Ascalon, report of the arrival of al-Afdal Shāhānshāh, 132; crusaders capture Arab herdsmen, 133, 134; defeat of the forces of al-Afdal, 135

'Azāz (Hazart), besieged by the Turks, 69; Godfrey marches to the aid of the apostate Turks, 69, 70

Baldwin of Boulogne, brother of Godfrey, captures Edessa, 73, 74

Beirut, arrival of the crusaders, 113

Bernard of Béziers, loses life, 33

Bertrand of Le Puy, reports a vision, 99

Bohemond, Norman crusader, son of Robert Guiscard, 22; supports Alexius, 24; makes diversionary march, 27; summons aid at Dorylaeum, 27; leads a skirmish against the Turks, 32; heads a foraging expedition into Hispania, 33; threatens to leave the siege of Antioch, 35; is offered Antioch by several leaders, 37; fights beside Raymond of Saint-Gilles against the Turks, 41, 42; orders gates of Antioch closed, 56, 57; seizes the citadel, 65; returns to Romania, 66; besieges Ma'arrat-an-Nu'mān, 76; incurs anger of the Provençals, 79; returns to Antioch, 80; seizes Antioch, 105

Bridge Gate, blocked by the Latins, 44

Bucca Torta, 113

Bucinat, castle on the route of the Provençals, 21

Budellus of Chartres, mounts walls of Antioch, 47

Bulgars, guard the Latins, 19

Caesarea, 114

Camela (Homs), crusaders purchase horses there, 84; sends gifts to the crusaders, 87